DISCOVERIES IN
SPACE SCIENCE

Exploring
Space

GENERAL EDITORS:
Giles Sparrow, Judith John, and Chris McNab

Cavendish
Square

New York

Published in 2016 by Cavendish Square Publishing, LLC
243 5th Avenue, Suite 136, New York, NY 10016

First Edition

Website: cavendishsq.com

CPSIA Compliance Information: Batch #CW16CSQ

Cataloging-in-Publication Data

Sparrow, Giles.
Exploring space / edited by Giles Sparrow, Judith John, and Chris McNab.
p. cm. — (Discoveries in space science)
Includes index.
ISBN 978-1-5026-1012-6 (hardcover) ISBN 978-1-5026-1013-3 (ebook)
1. Outer space — Exploration — Juvenile literature. 2. Astronauts — Juvenile literature.
I. Sparrow, Giles, 1970-. II. John, Judith. III. McNab, Chris, 1970-. IV. Title.
TL793.S63 2016
629.45—d23

Project Editor: Michael Spilling
Design: Hawes Design and Mark Batley
Picture Research: Terry Forshaw
Additional Text: Chris McNab and Judith John

All images are taken from the card set Secrets of the Universe (six volumes) published by International Masters Publishers AB, except the following: NASA/File:MAVENnMars.jpg/Wikimedia Commons, cover, 1; NASA/JPL/Corby Waste/File:Orbit insertion by Mars Reconnaissance Orbiter, artist's concept (PIA07242).jpg/Wikimedia Commons, 4–5; ISRO: 49–52 all; ESA: 68–71 all; ISRO: 66–67 all, 72–73 all.

Printed in the United States of America

TABLE OF CONTENTS

DISCOVERIES IN SPACE SCIENCE

Exploring Space

SATELLITES

On October 5, 1957, to US and world surprise, the Soviet Union launched *Sputnik 1* ("fellow traveler"), the first man-made object into orbit. *Sputnik 1* was nothing more than a bleeping radio transmitter, but many practical applications have since been found for artificial satellites. Today, well over two thousand are in Earth orbit. Satellites relay telephone calls, data, and television programs; observe changes in the environment, and provide accurate location data to GPS receivers, which have a wide range of civil and military applications. Purely military uses include monitoring ballistic missile launches, listening to enemy communications and electronic emissions, as well as imaging sites of military interest. The type of orbit is important. A geostationary orbit, in which the satellite remains over one point on Earth, allows communications to be relayed over most of the planet. Spy satellites and most other Earth-observing craft need to make moving orbits, passing over their targets for a short period each day. The modern world would barely function without satellites, and new launches will need to be made far into the foreseeable future.

UNMANNED SPUTNIKS

The Soviet Union amazed the world in 1957 when it launched the world's first artificial satellite, *Sputnik 1*. But this was just the first in a series of unmanned missions that ranged from scientific research to test flights for crewed space capsules and Venus-probe rocket stages. Together with three satellites that launched dogs into space, the success or failure of every mission was hidden behind the word "sputnik"—the name given to them by the Soviets to conceal their true purpose from the rest of the world.

UNMANNED LAUNCHES

Nickname	Real Name	Launch Date	Launch Vehicle	Reentry Date	Purpose
Sputnik 1	Object PS-1	October 4, 1957	8K71 (A-class)	January 4, 1958	Publicity
Sputnik 3	Object D-1	May 15, 1958	8A91 (A-class)	April 6, 1960	Scientific research
Sputnik 4	Object KS-1	May 15, 1960	8K72 (A-1 class)	October 15, 1965	Vostok capsule test
Sputnik 7	1VA No.1	February 4, 1961	8K78 (A-2-e class)	February 26, 1961	Venus probe launch
Sputnik 8	1VA No.2	February 12, 1961	8K78 (A-2-e class)	February 25, 1961	Venus probe launch

SPUTNIK 1
Launched from the Baikonur Cosmodrome, Soviet Union, on October 4, 1957, *Sputnik 1* (replica shown right) was the first human-made object to go into orbit around the Earth. The shiny sphere was carried into space by a modified R-7 booster. The satellite's orbit decayed after three months in space, at which point it burned up in the Earth's atmosphere.

SPUTNIK 3
The third Sputnik (right) was a geophysical satellite that sent back information about the Earth's atmosphere and near-Earth space. Powered by solar panels and zinc batteries, and measuring 140 x 68 inches (3.5 x 1.7 m) at the base, it was much larger than *Sputnik 1*.

nose cone

payload fairing

cylindrical main body of *Venera 1* probe

engine pump

support strut

main engine nozzle

instrument package

solar panel

propellant tank

secondary engine nozzles

SPUTNIK 4
This prototype Vostok capsule (right) was carried into orbit on *Sputnik 4* to be tested for spaceworthiness. Although the capsule suffered from malfunctions, the tests proved useful in ironing out design flaws, meaning that subsequent Sputnik missions were successful.

SPUTNIK 7 & 8
The *Venera 1* probe (left) was the first spacecraft to perform a flyby of the planet Venus in 1961. Launched on its mission earlier that same year by *Sputnik 8*, the cylindrical spacecraft was equipped with a high-gain antenna and a wide range of scientific instruments.

FIRST SHOTS

Sputnik 1 was one of the smallest and simplest spacecraft ever built. The 2-foot (60 centimeter)-wide, 184-pound (83 kilogram) aluminum alloy ball contained batteries, radio transmitters, and four long antennas, and transmitted a "beep...beep...beep" signal that could be received by amateur radio enthusiasts all over the world. But this simplicity of design was the secret to its success.

Sputnik 2, along with *Sputnik 5* and *6*, carried dogs into orbit to test the effects of space travel on animals. The next Sputnik without a living passenger was the 2,900-pound (1,315 kg) *Sputnik 3*. Larger and more sophisticated than *Sputnik 1*, it was originally intended to be the first Soviet satellite to reach space. Problems with its construction delayed the launch until May 1958—more than seven months after the first Sputnik.

A dozen instruments were fitted to *Sputnik 3* to study the Earth's upper atmosphere, magnetic field, and radiation belt, as well as any cosmic rays and micrometeoroids that might be found there. Small solar panels were built around its cone-shaped main body to provide power. *Sputnik 3* succeeded in transmitting data back to Earth until April 6, 1960, when its orbit decayed, causing it to burn up in the atmosphere.

The Soviet Union greeted the 1960s with the launch of *Sputnik 4*. This mission was the first test flight in space of the Vostok capsule—the spacecraft later used by Yuri Gagarin to become the first human in orbit. The engineers behind the new capsule called it Object KS-1 or "Spaceship-1." This first Vostok was a stripped-down, 7-foot 5-inch (2.2 meter)-wide test

capsule; it had no heat shield, no parachutes, and no ejection seat, and was intended to burn up in the atmosphere. On the outside of the ball-like capsule were a pair of small solar panels and some radio antennas. Strapped to the back of the Vostok was a service section containing thrusters and propellant tanks, more antennas, and heat control systems. The service section also housed Sun and Earth sensors for orientation of the capsule, and the main rocket engine used for reentry—but things went wrong when the time for reentry arrived. The capsule was facing the wrong direction when the rocket fired. Instead of descending, it shot into a higher orbit and didn't come down for five years.

Sputnik 7 and *8* were not actually satellites, but the upper stages of rocket launchers

designed to send Venera space probes to Venus. Built by Sergei Korolev's Design Bureau OKB-1, these "Block L" rocket stages relied upon a sophisticated motor that burned kerosene and liquid oxygen propellants during launches.

Block L was the first rocket engine designed to be fired while in orbit around the Earth. In the weightlessness of space, propellants tend to float around inside their tanks, which makes

it difficult to pump them into the engine. On *Sputnik 7* and *8*, small rockets were fired to force the propellants toward the bottom of their tanks and into the engine pumps. Due to a technical failure, *Sputnik 7* failed to release its payload. But on February 12, 1961, *Sputnik 8* did succeed in its mission—the upper rocket stage engine ignited in low orbit to successfully propel the *Venera 1* probe toward its destination.

SPY IN THE SKY

ON MAY 1, 1960, A U-2 SPY PLANE (RIGHT) FLOWN BY CIA PILOT GARY POWERS WAS SHOT DOWN BY A SURFACE-TO-AIR MISSILE OVER BAIKONUR COSMODROME IN THE SOVIET UNION. AT THE TIME, *SPUTNIK 4* WAS BEING PREPARED FOR LIFTOFF. THE SPACECRAFT WAS EVENTUALLY LAUNCHED TWO WEEKS LATER, ON MAY 15.

ANIMALS IN SPACE

Since the beginning of the Space Age in the 1950s, animals of many species have journeyed beyond the Earth's atmosphere. Not all of them have returned alive. Scientists have learned much from their animal helpers, but there is plenty of opposition—from other scientists as well as animal rights activists—to sending animals into space. For some, it is a crime; to others, it is a valuable research resource that helps mankind learn more about the universe and the effects of spending time traveling in space.

ANIMAL FLIGHTS

DATE	ANIMAL	MISSION	STUDY
Nov 1957	Dog Laika	*Sputnik 2*	Survivability of space flight
Dec 1960	Rhesus Monkey Sam	Little Joe Project	Effects of high-g acceleration
Jan 1961	Chimpanzee Ham	Mercury Redstone 2	Survivability of manned space flight
June 1973	Minnows	Skylab 3	Disorientation in the space environment
Aug 1973	Spiders	Skylab 3	Ability of spiders to adapt to zero-g
Mar 1982	Moths and Flies	Shuttle Mission STS-3	Insect flight motion study
Sept 1992	Frogs	Shuttle Mission STS-47	Effects of weightlessness on development of eggs
Oct 1993	Rats	Shuttle Mission STS-58	Effects of weightlessness
May 1994	Newts and Goldfish	Shuttle Mission STS-65	Effects of microgravity on embryos

SPACE BEASTS

Early in November 1957, a dog named Laika ("Little Lemon") became the first living being from the Earth to venture into space and orbit the planet. Laika's one-way mission aboard the Russian spacecraft *Sputnik 2* paved the way for manned spaceflight and marked the beginning of animal involvement in the Space Age.

A year later, two dogs, Belka ("Squirrel") and Strelka ("Little Arrow"), returned safely after a one-day flight on *Sputnik 5*. Strelka later gave birth to a litter of six puppies, one of which was given to President John F. Kennedy as a gift from the Soviet Union.

At the end of 1960, soon after the Sputnik mission, the US instigated its Little Joe animal-flight program. A rhesus monkey named Sam was sent into space as part of a series of animal flights designed to investigate the effects of high-g acceleration and to test the equipment that would later be used in manned missions.

These early animal pioneers proved that there was no danger in space that humans could not face—with a lot of good engineering and a little luck. Later research animals have helped us to understand some of the long-term effects of weightlessness on bodies that have evolved to function in a powerful gravity field.

On short journeys, such effects are minor. But even a week or two in space is enough to affect heart muscles, depress immune systems, and distort coordination and balance. A little longer and astronauts begin to suffer from osteoporosis, a weakening of the bones. This weakening is caused when their bodies recycle structural bone material, which is apparently no longer needed because of the absence of gravity.

Although some Russian cosmonauts have lived for many months on the Mir space station, they have needed considerable time to recover upon their return to Earth. Future missions to Mars, or the construction of space colonies, are likely to put the human body under considerable strain.

Spaceborne animals have helped to quantify at least some of the consequences of zero gravity (known as zero g). But such experiments have their opponents, too. Some scientists argue that the stress of weightlessness itself is enough to invalidate the results of some animal experiments, and that most animal anatomies are not close enough to our own for them to serve as testbeds. Also, creatures such as mice and rats are too short-lived for scientists to gain much long-term data from them. And animal well-being is taken seriously. The Bion—a long-term collaboration between the US and Russia—insists that animals involved in missions are retired soon after to live out the remainder of their natural lives in comfort.

LAIKA: SPACE PIONEER

OCTOBER 1957
THE RUSSIAN MONGREL LAIKA UNDERGOES A PROGRAM OF EXTENSIVE TRAINING TO ACCLIMATIZE HER TO CONFINED SPACES, HIGH ACCELERATION FORCES, AND ENGINE NOISE THAT SHE WILL EXPERIENCE ON HER VOYAGE.

NOVEMBER 3, 1957
SPUTNIK 2 IS LAUNCHED INTO ORBIT. THE TOP SECTION CONTAINS INSTRUMENTS TO MEASURE RADIATION, THE MIDDLE HOLDS THE RADIO CAPSULE, AND BELOW IS THE COMPARTMENT CONTAINING LAIKA.

NOVEMBER 10, 1957
LAIKA DIES AFTER RUNNING OUT OF OXYGEN. *SPUTNIK 2* CONTINUES TO ORBIT FOR MORE THAN SIX MONTHS. LAIKA AND THE CRAFT BURN UP ON REENTRY INTO THE ATMOSPHERE.

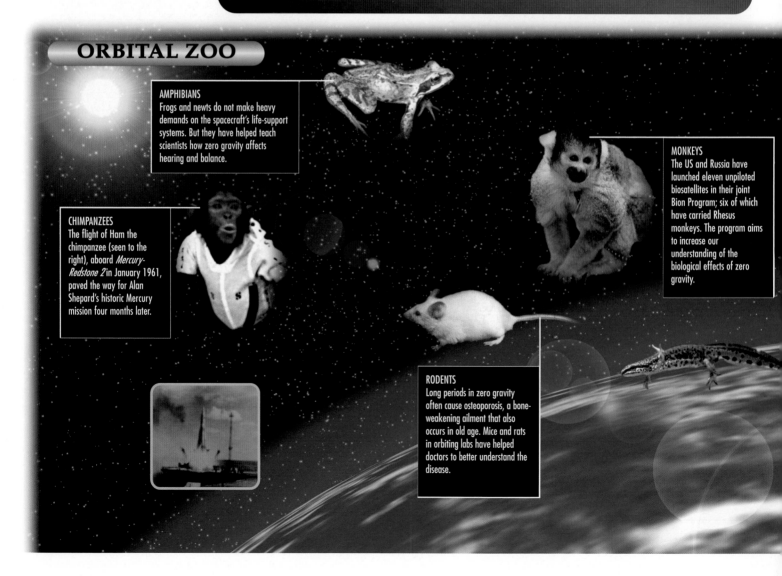

ORBITAL ZOO

AMPHIBIANS
Frogs and newts do not make heavy demands on the spacecraft's life-support systems. But they have helped teach scientists how zero gravity affects hearing and balance.

CHIMPANZEES
The flight of Ham the chimpanzee (seen to the right), aboard *Mercury-Redstone 2* in January 1961, paved the way for Alan Shepard's historic Mercury mission four months later.

MONKEYS
The US and Russia have launched eleven unpiloted biosatellites in their joint Bion Program; six of which have carried Rhesus monkeys. The program aims to increase our understanding of the biological effects of zero gravity.

RODENTS
Long periods in zero gravity often cause osteoporosis, a bone-weakening ailment that also occurs in old age. Mice and rats in orbiting labs have helped doctors to better understand the disease.

EXPLORER 1

During the late 1950s, the United States and the Soviet Union carried their rivalry into Earth orbit. The Soviets took an early lead by successfully launching two Sputnik satellites. The US, uneasy at the thought of Soviet space hardware tracking over North America, redoubled its efforts and responded with *Explorer 1* early in 1958. But the first American satellite did more than save face for the US in the Cold War. Once in orbit, the onboard instruments discovered belts of radiation in the Earth's magnetosphere.

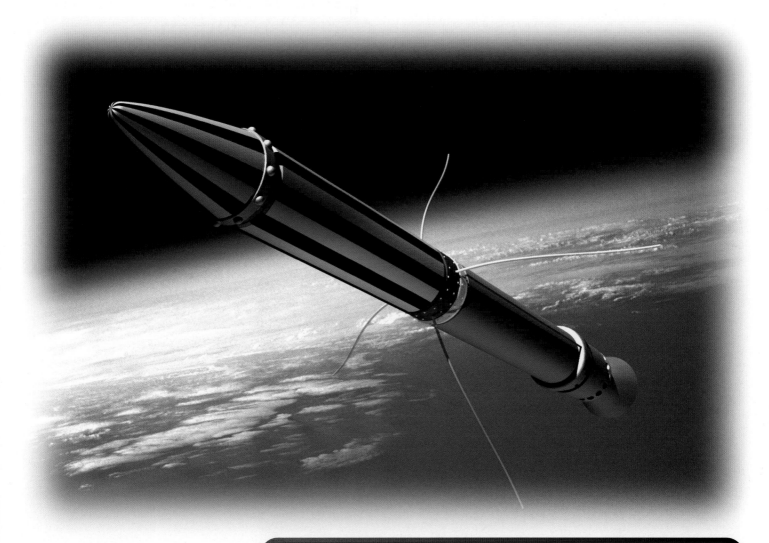

EXPLORER 1 SPECIFICATIONS

DIMENSIONS	80 IN (203 CM) LONG, 6 INCHES (15 CM) IN DIAMETER
WEIGHT	30.66 LB (13.9 KG)
LAUNCH DATE/TIME	JANUARY 31, 1958, 10:47 P.M. EST
LAUNCH SITE	CAPE CANAVERAL, FLORIDA
LAUNCH VEHICLE	JUPITER-C
ORBITAL INFORMATION	PERIGEE: 1,575 MILES (2,534 KM) APOGEE: 224 MILES (360 KM)
	INCLINATION: 33.24 DEGREES PERIOD: 114.9 MINUTES

INTO ORBIT

After the Soviet Union launched *Sputnik 1*, the world's first artificial satellite, opinion was divided in the US as to the significance of the event. Did this little metal ball, spinning and beeping its way around the globe, really present a threat to the western world? President Eisenhower, in public, was on the side of the skeptics. But privately, after a U-2 spy plane was shot down over the Soviet Union, he saw the potential of satellite technology as a safe way of peeking over the Iron Curtain.

Certainly Eisenhower's military advisers saw Sputnik as a potential threat to American security, and their fears were voiced on Capitol Hill by Senator Stuart Symington. "Unless our defense policies are promptly changed, the Soviets will move from superiority to supremacy," Symington warned. The US military wanted more resources for a reconnaissance satellite program.

Meanwhile, the Soviets surged

ahead once more. On November 3, 1957, *Sputnik 2* was launched carrying Laika the dog—the first living being in space. *Sputnik 2* raised the stakes. It was suddenly clear that the Soviet space effort was looking far beyond the obvious military advantages of being able to send missiles into orbit. They wanted to put a man into space—an achievement with extraordinary propaganda value in a war of ideas between competing superpowers. Smaller nations might well be tempted to line up behind the winner of the Space Race.

The first US satellite launch attempt failed on December 6 of that same year, when a Vanguard rocket exploded two seconds into its flight. But this left the field clear for rocket pioneer Wernher von Braun. On January 31, 1958, a four-stage Jupiter-C launched from Cape Canaveral with an upgraded Redstone rocket as the first stage. Inside was *Explorer 1*, which was launched into an orbit measuring 224 by 1,575 miles (360 by 2,534 km).

Two hours later, Eisenhower

told the American people, "The United States has successfully placed a scientific satellite in orbit around the Earth. This is part of our participation in the International Geophysical Year." The International Geophysical Year (IGY) was a global venture, bringing together scientists from sixty-six countries to investigate Earth's climate and atmosphere.

Explorer 1 made a sensational contribution to the IGY, thanks to the onboard Geiger tube radiation detector that discovered belts of intense radiation girdling the Earth. The instrument was designed by James Van Allen, one of the architects of the IGY. Fittingly, the radiation belts still bear his name.

MEDIA FRENZY

Explorer 1 aroused intense media interest. As Van Allen himself recalled of one press conference, "Although it was 1:30 in the morning, there was still a huge crowd of reporters waiting around." But the story was more about how the US had caught up with the Soviets than about the satellite's remarkable scientific achievements.

WIRED

The Explorer series continues to this day. *Explorer 75*, the "Wide-Field Infrared Explorer," or WIRE (right), was launched on March 4, 1999, and carried an infrared imaging telescope. Unfortunately, an accident shortly after launch meant that the spacecraft quickly grew too warm. The telescope could not be used and the mission was declared a loss.

MISSION DIARY: *EXPLORER 1*

1957
Work steps up on the development of *Explorer 1* (right) at the US Army research facility known as the Jet Propulsion Laboratory in Pasadena, California.

November 3, 1957
The Soviet Union launches *Sputnik 2* with Laika on board.

December 6, 1957
Unsuccessful launch of first the US satellite.

January 29, 1958
Scheduled launch of *Explorer 1* is aborted due to high winds in the upper atmosphere.

January 30, 1958
Launch postponed a second time. The satellite and its launcher remain on the launchpad (right).

January 31, 1958, 10:47 P.M. EST
Explorer 1 lifts off from Cape Canaveral (far right).

10:55:05 P.M.
Explorer 1 reaches Earth orbit.

February 1, 1958, 1:00 A.M.
President Eisenhower announces "the United States has successfully placed a scientific Earth satellite in orbit around the Earth."

March 31, 1970, 5:47 A.M. EST
Explorer 1 burns up during its reentry into Earth's atmosphere.

ORBITAL PATH
Explorer 1's simple orbital path carried it around the globe once every 107 minutes. The satellite continued its transmissions until May 23, 1958.

LAST CHECK
Engineers check *Explorer 1* prior to launch. As well as Van Allen's Geiger counter, the satellite carried instruments for detecting the presence of micrometeoroids.

LOUD AND CLEAR
Confirmation that *Explorer 1* has successfully entered Earth orbit, as seen on the screens of Goldstone Tracking Station in California.

low-power transmitter

temperature probe

radiation detection package

high-power transmitter

turnstile antenna wire

EXPLORER 1 IN ORBIT

LAUNCHING SATELLITES

A satellite's journey into space usually involves several phases, each with its own hazards. First, the launching rocket places its payload in low Earth orbit. Then a rocket burn sends the satellite out along an elliptical transfer orbit. Finally, another rocket motor, strapped to the satellite or built into it, puts the craft permanently into its planned orbit. Such maneuvers are all routine for rocket engineers. But a single failure at any point can turn an expensive piece of technology into a piece of space junk.

ORBITAL MILESTONES

First satellite launch into orbit	October 4, 1957 (*Sputnik 1*)
First US satellite launch into orbit	February 1, 1958 (*Explorer 1*)
First launch into polar orbit	February 28, 1959 (*Discoverer 1*)
First launch of several satellites at once	June 22, 1960 (*Transit 2A*, *Sunray*)
First landing of a satellite from orbit	August 18, 1960 (*Discoverer 14*)
First commercial communications satellite launch	July 10, 1962 (*Telstar 1*)
First launch into geostationary orbit	August 19, 1964 (*Syncom 3*)
First Shuttle retrieval of a satellite	November 16, 1984 (*Palapa B-2* & *Westar 6*)

KICK START

The first part of a satellite's journey to its working orbit usually begins with a rocket launch that leaves the spacecraft at least 80 miles (129 km) above the Earth and moving at around 17,000 miles per hour (27,500 kmh)—orbital velocity. At this height, no orbit is stable. The Earth's atmosphere is still thick enough for its drag to bring the satellite down within a few days or weeks. Most spacecraft are designed to work from a higher altitude, from a few hundred miles for most observational satellites to the 22,700-mile (36,500 km) geostationary orbit that is now the home of much communications equipment.

To get the satellite to its planned orbit, at least two more rocket burns are necessary. Both must be made in strict accordance with the laws of orbital mechanics. The first takes place at the satellite's perigee—where it is closest to the Earth's surface and moving at its fastest. The extra speed sends the craft on a transfer orbit that joins its original low orbit with its planned final orbit. This is usually performed by the perigee kick motor (PKM), which may be part of the launching rocket or the satellite itself.

The next burn takes place when the satellite reaches the apogee of its transfer orbit—its highest point above the Earth. The apogee kick motor (AKM), usually mounted on board the satellite, increases the spacecraft's speed once more, and converts the long ellipse of the transfer orbit into the near-perfect circle usually required for its permanent, final orbit.

GIVEN A BOOST

Without the help of the AKM to boost speed, the satellite would simply fall back to the low point in its orbit where it fired the PKM. The extra thrust gives the orbit a new and much higher perigee, leaving the satellite where its designers intended. Onboard thrusters may make a few minor course and altitude adjustments.

Next, the electricity-producing solar panels are unveiled, antennas unfold, instruments extend, and communications dishes open up and snap into place—although some of this apparatus may have deployed earlier during the transfer orbit to enable Mission Control to talk to the satellite or to run the satellite's electrical systems. With the satellite operational in its final orbit, the launch vehicle is destroyed—unless the satellite has been carried into space by a reusable craft, which returns to Earth on completion of a mission.

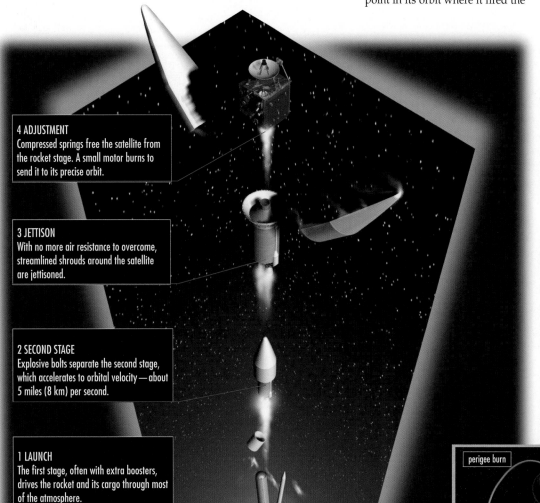

4 ADJUSTMENT
Compressed springs free the satellite from the rocket stage. A small motor burns to send it to its precise orbit.

3 JETTISON
With no more air resistance to overcome, streamlined shrouds around the satellite are jettisoned.

2 SECOND STAGE
Explosive bolts separate the second stage, which accelerates to orbital velocity — about 5 miles (8 km) per second.

1 LAUNCH
The first stage, often with extra boosters, drives the rocket and its cargo through most of the atmosphere.

INTO ORBIT

The journey from launchpad to final orbit involves several rocket firings, each with a precise purpose. Usually, the spacecraft will travel from low Earth orbit to a higher station by means of a transfer orbit. The journey depends on accurate timing: a small error can leave the satellite hopelessly lost.

HARD EVIDENCE

MOTORING
A satellite reaches low Earth orbit (LEO) after a rocket or Shuttle launch. Then, a perigee kick motor fires to send the satellite into a transfer orbit. Finally, an apogee kick motor (example below) fires to project the satellite into its final orbit. Some perigee and apogee rocket firings are achieved by the upper stage of the launch rocket — for example, the Russian Proton's Block DM or the US Atlas rocket's Centaur.

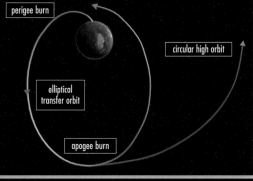

peerigee burn

circular high orbit

elliptical transfer orbit

apogee burn

Placed by its booster in an initial low Earth orbit, a satellite first makes a perigee burn at the lowest point. The burn sends the satellite climbing into an elliptical transfer orbit. At the apogee — the highest point — a second burn pushes the satellite into a much higher, possibly geostationary, orbit.

TELSTAR 1

One day in July 1962, scientists at a receiving station in France beamed with delight when they heard "The Star-Spangled Banner" and saw a picture of the American flag on a TV screen. They had just received the first-ever transatlantic TV relay, transmitted from the United States by the new Telstar satellite. Although the experimental satellite could only broadcast during a limited period each day, its pioneering transmissions paved the way for a revolution in international communications.

TELSTAR 1

LAUNCH DATE	JULY 10, 1962	ORBITAL PARAMETERS	586 MILES (943 KM) x 3,499 MILES (5,631 KM)
LAUNCH VEHICLE	DELTA BOOSTER	ORBITAL INCLINATION	44.8°
LAUNCH SITE	CAPE CANAVERAL	FREQUENCIES	UPLINK: 6,390 MHz
WEIGHT	171 LB (77.5 KG)		DOWNLINK: 4,170 MHz

MOVING PICTURES

As early as October 1945, science fiction writer Arthur C. Clarke had discussed the possibility of worldwide television and radio broadcasts using spacecraft as orbiting relays. In Clarke's model, space stations would travel in geostationary orbit, providing total coverage of the Earth for television and radio.

By 1962, the technology required to maintain stations in space was still on the drawing board, but John R. Pierce and his team at AT&T's Bell Laboratories were designing a simpler, less costly kind of relay—the artificial satellite Telstar. Pierce's strategy was ambitious. It called for "a system of 40 satellites in polar orbits, and 15 in equatorial orbits…and about 25 ground stations, so placed as to provide global coverage."

Truly worldwide broadcasts, though, would require worldwide cooperation. The reality of Cold War politics made this impossible, and the goal of the Telstar project was simplified: put a satellite into low Earth orbit and use it to transmit television pictures across the Atlantic.

AT&T paid NASA $3 million to launch *Telstar 1* on July 10, 1962. The spacecraft was placed into a high, elliptical orbit, where it immediately encountered an unforeseen hazard. The day before launch, the United States had detonated Starfish, a powerful nuclear weapon that exploded high above the atmosphere. Radiation from the blast would take its toll on Telstar in the months to come. But in the hours after launch, the Telstar team stayed glued to their television sets, awaiting the first intercontinental telecast.

ATLANTIC LINKUP

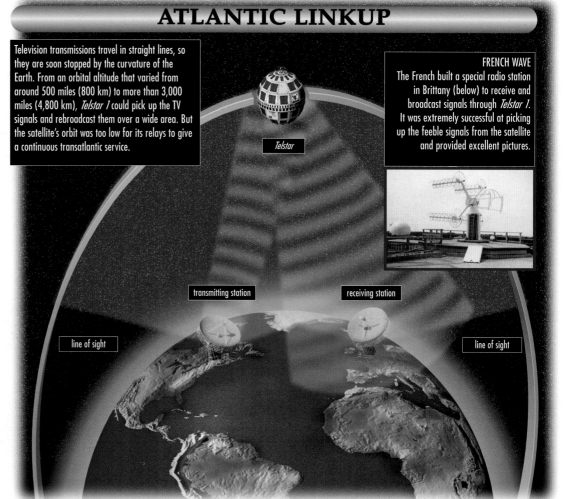

Television transmissions travel in straight lines, so they are soon stopped by the curvature of the Earth. From an orbital altitude that varied from around 500 miles (800 km) to more than 3,000 miles (4,800 km), *Telstar 1* could pick up the TV signals and rebroadcast them over a wide area. But the satellite's orbit was too low for its relays to give a continuous transatlantic service.

Telstar

FRENCH WAVE
The French built a special radio station in Brittany (below) to receive and broadcast signals through *Telstar 1*. It was extremely successful at picking up the feeble signals from the satellite and provided excellent pictures.

transmitting station   receiving station

line of sight   line of sight

WAVES ACROSS THE WORLD

In Andover, Maine, Bell Laboratories flew the American flag for its broadcast. In Pleumeur-Bodou in Brittany, France, technicians were poised to transmit recordings of an actor, a singer, and a guitarist. And at Goonhilly Down in Cornwall, England, the control room was ready to receive the first images. But all three stations had to wait

for Telstar to reach the right place. The satellite's low orbit meant that there was only a limited period during which it was above the horizon—and in the line of sight—for both European and US transceiver stations. Transatlantic TV was only possible for 102 minutes each day.

At the appointed moment, France picked up Old Glory. Technical problems delayed British reception, and it was late in the night before the BBC

received pictures of AT&T chairman Frederick Kappel reading a statement. They couldn't hear him because the sound had failed.

Despite technical glitches, *Telstar 1* was an outstanding achievement, blazing a trail for the extraordinary growth in global telecommunication. Arthur C. Clarke is the author of many science fiction classics, but his "extraterrestrial relays" have become a reality.

MISSION DIARY: *TELSTAR 1*

1960 AT&T BEGINS RESEARCH AND DEVELOPMENT FOR A SATELLITE COMMUNICATIONS SYSTEM: *TELSTAR 1* (RIGHT). **1961** J.R. PIERCE OF BELL LABORATORIES, AN AT&T SUBSIDIARY, ESTIMATES COST OF TELSTAR PROJECT AT **$500** MILLION. **JULY 24** CONCERNED ABOUT THE PROSPECT OF AN AT&T MONOPOLY IN TELECOMMUNICATIONS, PRESIDENT KENNEDY ANNOUNCES MEASURES TO GUARANTEE COMPETITION AND ADVOCATES INTERNATIONAL PARTNERSHIP IN THE FIELD. **JULY 9, 1962** THE US MILITARY DETONATES A HUGE

THERMONUCLEAR TEST WEAPON, STARFISH, AT HIGH ALTITUDE WITHOUT ADVANCE WARNING. **JULY 10, 1962** *TELSTAR 1* LAUNCHED INTO ELLIPTICAL EARTH ORBIT FROM CAPE CANAVERAL IN FLORIDA. **JULY 11, 1962** *TELSTAR 1* RELAYS TV PICTURES FROM A STATION IN ANDOVER, MAINE, TO A RECEIVER ON FRANCE'S EAST COAST. FRANCE RETURN PICTURES OF AN ACTOR, A SINGER, AND GUITARIST (ABOVE). BRITAIN PICKS UP SIGNAL LATER, AT GOONHILLY RECEIVING STATION (FAR RIGHT). **AUGUST 31** US GOVERNMENT PASSES COMMUNICATION

SATELLITE ACT. IT SETS UP A FEDERALLY FUNDED SATELLITE COMMUNICATIONS CORPORATION, COMSAT. **OCTOBER** TELSTAR 1, ALREADY DAMAGED BY ATMOSPHERIC RADIATION FROM THE US NUCLEAR TEST IN JULY, IS FURTHER COMPROMISED BY A MATCHING SOVIET NUCLEAR TEST. GROUND CONTROLLERS MANAGE TO CARRY OUT SOME REMOTE REPAIRS. **DECEMBER** *TELSTAR 1* FINALLY CEASES TO OPERATE. **MAY 7, 1963** *TELSTAR 2* LAUNCHED. COMMUNICATIONS RESUME SUCCESSFULLY.

EARLY WARNING SATELLITES

T he chilling words "Missile launch alert!" quicken the hearts of military personnel around the world. They mean that some form of attack could be under way—and if it is, every second of early warning is invaluable. Missile early warning is the mission of the United States military's Defense Support Program (DSP). Providing worldwide coverage, the DSP uses a network of at least five satellites in geosynchronous orbit to monitor the Earth, watching for space and missile launches.

CURRENT DSP SATELLITES

PRIMARY MISSION	STRATEGIC AND TACTICAL MISSILE LAUNCH DETECTION	POWER GENERATION	SOLAR ARRAYS GENERATING 1,485 WATTS (SATELLITE USES 1,274 WATTS)
ORBITAL ALTITUDE	22,233 MILES (35,780 KM)	FIRST DEPLOYED	NOVEMBER 6, 1970
HEIGHT	32.8 FT (10 M) ON ORBIT, 28 FT (8.5 M) AT LAUNCH	UNIT COST	APPROXIMATELY $250 MILLION EACH
		SATELLITES IN PROGRAM	23
DIAMETER	22 FT (6.7 M) ON ORBIT, 13.7 FT (4.1 M) AT LAUNCH	CONTRACTOR TEAM	TRW AND AEROJET ELECTRONICS SYSTEMS
WEIGHT	5,250 LB (2,381 KG)		

TIMELY WARNINGS

The US military's Defense Support Program (DSP) is a survivable and reliable satellite-based system that uses infrared sensors to detect missile and space launches and nuclear detonations. The early warning program began in 1966, but the first launch of a satellite didn't occur until November 6, 1970. Since then, DSP satellites have fed a constant stream of warning data, 24 hours a day, 365 days a year, to the Missile Warning Center at Cheyenne Mountain, Colorado, via ground stations as far away as Australia and Germany.

As the DSP program progressed, the satellite went through five major design changes, each one increasing its capabilities. Phase 1 satellites had 2,048 sensor elements—optimized to detect a single infrared wavelength—and a planned three-year life span. By the fifth design, DSPs had six thousand sensors on two wavelengths and seven- to nine-year lifetimes. They were also hardened against laser jamming and nuclear attack, and they were capable of detecting any imminent physical threat from an attack satellite and maneuvering themselves out of harm's way.

The DSP proved its worth during Operation Desert Storm, in the Gulf War of 1991. Originally designed to detect strategic threats against the continental United States, the DSP satellites turned their attention to the Persian Gulf and detected Iraqi ballistic missiles being launched against the US-led coalition forces.

SCUDBUSTERS

The DSP's superb operational performance during Operation Desert Storm demonstrated that the system, although designed to detect intercontinental missile launches, could also provide significant early warning against comparatively small tactical missiles. Every Scud missile launch made during the Gulf War was detected within seconds of liftoff. Warnings were relayed to civilian populations and coalition forces, including Patriot missile defense batteries, in Saudi Arabia and Israel.

Without a doubt, the Defense Support Program was also a key factor in America's winning the Cold War. Because of the DSP's global satellite coverage, no missile launch, no matter where it came from, could go unnoticed. No aggressor could launch an attack without being detected—and they knew it. The program continues to be one of the US military's most successful programs ever.

WATCHING FROM ABOVE

A DSP satellite spins at about 6 revolutions per minute (rpm) so that its detector systems can make continuous scans of the Earth below. Its magnetic plasma and synchronous orbit particle analyzers monitor electrical and radiation conditions in the atmosphere.

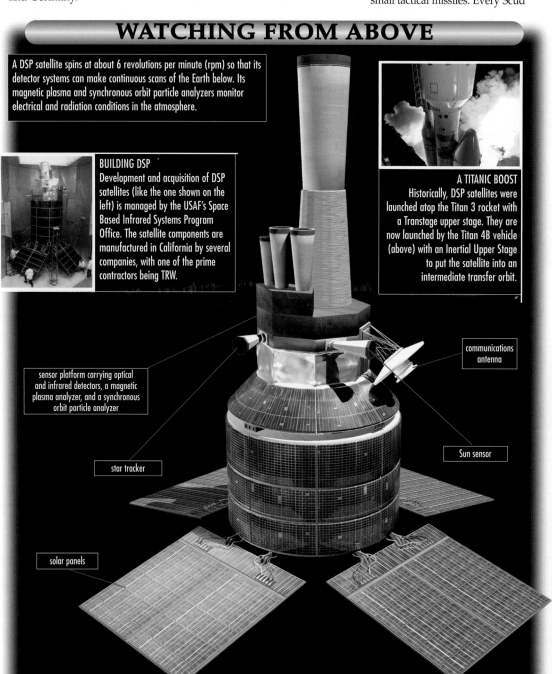

BUILDING DSP
Development and acquisition of DSP satellites (like the one shown on the left) is managed by the USAF's Space Based Infrared Systems Program Office. The satellite components are manufactured in California by several companies, with one of the prime contractors being TRW.

A TITANIC BOOST
Historically, DSP satellites were launched atop the Titan 3 rocket with a Transtage upper stage. They are now launched by the Titan 4B vehicle (above) with an Inertial Upper Stage to put the satellite into an intermediate transfer orbit.

sensor platform carrying optical and infrared detectors, a magnetic plasma analyzer, and a synchronous orbit particle analyzer

communications antenna

Sun sensor

star tracker

solar panels

HARD EVIDENCE

WATCHING THE WORLD
The current DSP satellites use sensor arrays of 6,000 lead sulfide and mercury cadmium telluride elements to detect infrared radiation. These sensors detect and track the exhaust heat generated by ballistic missiles (above right) and are sensitive enough to detect military jet aircraft operating on afterburners. Additionally, DSPs carry optical sensors that can detect nuclear detonations and large meteoroids entering the atmosphere. The main sensor barrel of a DSP satellite is tilted 7.5 degrees to the side and the vehicle spins as it travels around its orbit, so the sensors sweep out a cone-like pattern to cover a wide area.

PAYLOAD

DSP SATELLITE NUMBER 16 (ABOVE) WAS THE FIRST UNCLASSIFIED DSP LAUNCH AND SO FAR THE FIRST AND ONLY LAUNCH OF A DSP SATELLITE BY THE SPACE SHUTTLE. THE SHUTTLE *DISCOVERY* DEPLOYED THE SATELLITE ON NOVEMBER 25, 1991, ON THE SECOND DAY OF THE STS-44 MISSION. THE SATELLITE WAS BOOSTED TO GEOSYNCHRONOUS ORBIT BY THE NASA-DEVELOPED INERTIAL UPPER STAGE AND WAS THE ONLY DSP PUBLICLY GIVEN A NAME — *LIBERTY*.

SPY SATELLITES

Insurgent movements in Afghanistan, troop deployments in Iran, and the drug barons of Colombia are among the many targets being spied on by military satellites of the US, Russia, and several other countries. These photoreconnaissance satellites usually fly at an altitude of 100 miles (160 km) or more above the ground and at speeds of over 17,000 miles per hour (27,000 kmh), but they produce highly detailed images that can reveal even such relatively small objects as individual people—and their abilities are constantly being improved. Both visible and infrared images can now be transmitted.

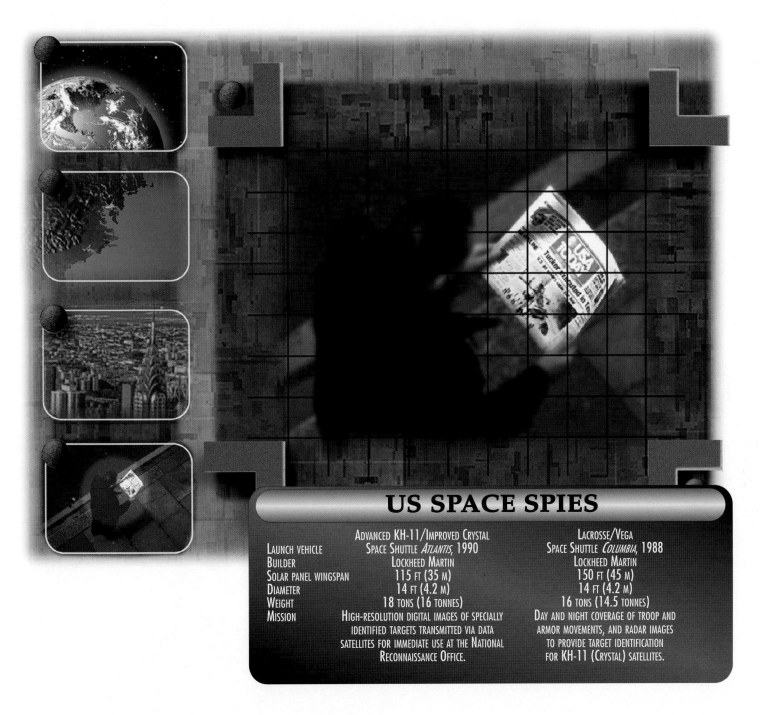

US SPACE SPIES

	Advanced KH-11/Improved Crystal	Lacrosse/Vega
Launch vehicle	Space Shuttle *Atlantis*, 1990	Space Shuttle *Columbia*, 1988
Builder	Lockheed Martin	Lockheed Martin
Solar panel wingspan	115 ft (35 m)	150 ft (45 m)
Diameter	14 ft (4.2 m)	14 ft (4.2 m)
Weight	18 tons (16 tonnes)	16 tons (14.5 tonnes)
Mission	High-resolution digital images of specially identified targets transmitted via data satellites for immediate use at the National Reconnaissance Office.	Day and night coverage of troop and armor movements, and radar images to provide target identification for KH-11 (Crystal) satellites.

SPIES IN THE SKY

Spying from above is nothing new—balloons were used to spy on enemy positions during many nineteenth-century wars, and aircraft have been used for reconnaissance since as early as World War I. The coming of space technology and the ability to get satellites into orbit—out of range of missiles—made the spy satellite a logical development in reconnaissance. The ideal orbit is one that takes the satellite over the poles of the Earth at a relatively low altitude of about 200 miles (320 km). At that height, seventeen orbits—covering the whole of the Earth— can be flown in a single day.

The US flew its first spy satellites under the name Discoverer in 1959. These top-secret craft, code-named Corona by the CIA, first became operational in 1960 and took pictures on film. The film was then returned to Earth for analysis in a reentry capsule. The Soviet Union launched its first spy satellite in 1962. Code-named Zenit, this also returned a recoverable film capsule.

Hundreds of spy satellites have been launched since the early 1960s. In addition to the US and Russian programs, spy satellite missions launched by other countries include those of China and Israel, and a joint European venture by France, Spain, and Italy.

DIGITAL SYSTEMS

The smallest ground-based object that could be seen in the early satellite images was the size of a house. Today, the technology is improving so much that spy satellites could soon be reading the headlines on a newspaper.

Film capsules are being replaced by high-resolution, multispectral digital systems that take both visible-light and infrared pictures, and transmit these images back to ground stations. Infrared photography produces images of heat patterns, so it can be used by night as well as day, and radar reconnaissance satellites can record images day or night through even the thickest cloud cover.

The digital images recorded by US satellites are transmitted to the National Reconnaissance Office in Washington, DC, via military communications satellites and NASA's Tracking and Data Relay Satellites, for analysis.

KH-11
The first of the US KH-11 (Crystal) series of spy satellites was launched from the Space Shuttle in 1990. Since then, several others have been launched on Titan 4 rockets. The satellites in this series are equipped with digital multispectral imaging systems, as well as electronic intelligence sensors.

SHUTTLE SPY

A SPACE SHUTTLE MISSION LAUNCHED IN NOVEMBER 1991 DEPLOYED A MISSILE EARLY WARNING SATELLITE AND ALSO CARRIED OUT EXPERIMENTS CALLED "TERRA SCOUT" AND "MILITARY MAN IN SPACE." THESE INVOLVED THE FIRST AMERICAN SPACE SPY, THOMAS HENNAN (RIGHT), WHO TESTED THE EFFECTIVENESS OF HUMAN RECONNAISSANCE FROM SPACE USING HIGH-RESOLUTION SENSORS AND CAMERAS.

MISSILE GAP

ONE OF THE FIRST SPY SATELLITE IMAGES, TAKEN BY *DISCOVERER 14* IN 1960 AS PART OF THE CORONA PROGRAM, SHOWED A MILITARY AIRFIELD IN NORTHEAST RUSSIA. THE PROGRAM SHOWED THAT, DESPITE THE CLAIMS OF SOVIET PREMIER NIKITA KRUSCHEV, THE SOVIET UNION DID NOT HAVE MORE INTERCONTINENTAL BALLISTIC MISSILES DEPLOYED THAN THE US DID. CORONA IMAGES BROUGHT THE ESTIMATE OF THE NUMBER OF MISSILES THEN IN THE SOVIET UNION'S NUCLEAR ARMORY DOWN FROM HUNDREDS TO TENS.

HIGH RES
Russia operates Zenit, Yantar, and Kometa satellites that return high-resolution images on film in recoverable capsules. Since the collapse of the Soviet Union, some of these images have been sold commercially. They show that the cameras could see details as small as 3 feet (1 m) across.

KOSMOS/ZENIT
The Soviet Union attempted to conceal the launches of its Zenit spy satellites by making them part of its Kosmos program of scientific satellites. This Zenit satellite carries a number of flask-like recoverable film capsules that are periodically dropped back to Earth. Newer versions transmit digital images directly back to ground stations.

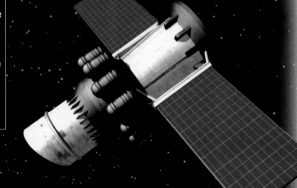

EUROPEAN SPACE SPY
Europe's first military spy satellite, *Helios 1*, was launched in 1995 aboard an Ariane rocket. Helios was based on the successful Spot commercial remote-sensing satellites, one of which took this infrared image of Baghdad, the capital of Iraq.

SCIENTIFIC SATELLITES

Every minute of every day, scientific satellites look both inward and outward, studying everything from deforestation and the hole in the Earth's ozone layer to exploding stars and supermassive black holes at the hearts of galaxies. Since the dawn of the Space Age, the world's space agencies have launched hundreds of scientific satellites into Earth orbit and sent scores more to study the other bodies of the solar system. Future probes will look deeper into our own planet—and into the farthest reaches of time and space.

SATELLITE MISSIONS

Satellite	Mission
Landsat 7	Monitor crop resources, minerals, and forests
TOPEX/ Poseidon	Monitor global ocean circulation and sea levels
SoHO	Study the structure and physics of the Sun
Imager	Produce 3-D images of Earth's magnetosphere
Hubble Space Telescope	Optical ultraviolet, infrared observations of the universe
Chandra X-Ray Observatory	Study hot, violent objects and events
Extreme Ultraviolet Explorer	Study white dwarfs and other objects
Mars Global Surveyor	Map the surface of Mars and study Martian climate
NEAR Shoemaker	Map the surface and chemical content of asteroid Eros
Galileo	Study Jupiter and its moons
Cassini	Rendezvous with Saturn

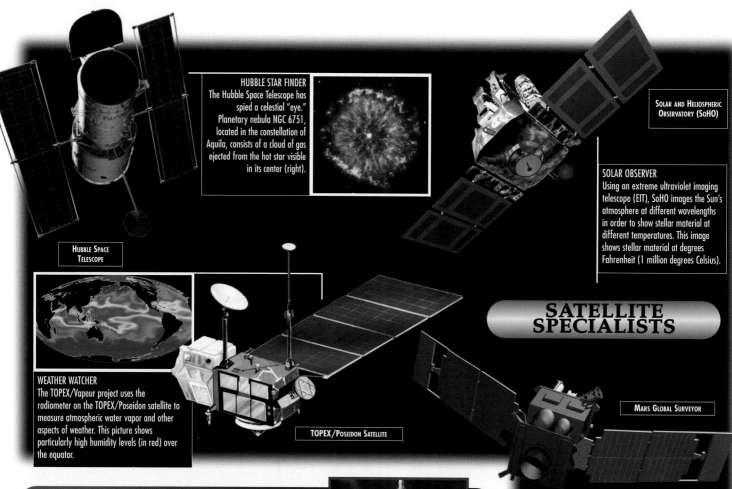

LAB PARTNERS

May 9, 2000, is a good example of a busy day around the solar system. From Earth orbit, *Landsat 7* surveyed an out-of-control wildfire that was advancing on Los Alamos, New Mexico. *Landsat 7*'s optical and infrared images helped firefighters assess the size and movement of the blaze and pinpoint hot spots. At the same time, the Tropical Rainfall Measuring Mission was peering through the clouds to measure the temperature of the ocean surface. Such measurements can help scientists understand and predict climate changes, such as the El Niño and La Niña events. Far from Earth, the NEAR Shoemaker spacecraft was orbiting less than 30 miles (50 km) above the surface of 433 Eros, a large asteroid. And a

half-billion miles away, the *Galileo* satellite was preparing for another encounter with Ganymede, the largest moon of Jupiter.

These and many other scientific satellites are extending our knowledge of Earth and of humanity's impact on our planet, as well as the interaction between the Sun, the Earth, and the cosmos—from the Moon and planets to the very edge of the visible universe.

Satellites have conducted scientific missions since the very beginning of the Space Age. *Explorer 1*, the first American satellite, discovered the radiation belts that encircle Earth in 1958. Since then, the world's space agencies have launched hundreds of satellites designed to expand our understanding of physics, astronomy, meteorology,

oceanography, and many other fields. Earth resources satellites locate mineral deposits, monitor deforestation, and measure ozone depletion and global warming. City planners use satellite data to help draft new zoning laws, and satellite images have been used as evidence in lawsuits against industrial polluters.

Several craft are studying the interaction of the Sun's magnetic field and the solar wind—a steady flow of charged particles from the Sun's outer atmosphere—with Earth's magnetic field. Outbursts from the Sun can knock out power grids, disrupt radio communications, and zap orbiting satellites, so understanding this interaction is especially important for our progressively more technological society.

Beyond Earth, probes have scanned the Moon and every planet except the dwarf planet Pluto (which NASA's *New Horizons* reached in 2015), plus several asteroids and comets. They have discovered ancient river valleys on Mars, possible oceans beneath the icy crust of Jupiter's moon Europa, and giant volcanoes on Io, another Jovian moon. Observatories in Earth orbit have discovered the "seeds" from which stars and galaxies grew, imaged powerful jets of hot gas squirting away from black holes, and found evidence of a "dark energy" that may be forcing the universe to expand ever faster.

These missions continue to push back the boundaries of the known universe, expand our knowledge of our own world, and increase our understanding of our place in the cosmos.

WEATHER SATELLITES

For as long as people have looked at clouds in the sky, there have been people who have tried to predict what tomorrow's weather will be. Forecasting the weather is still a tricky business, but accurate information about it is crucial to modern life—advance knowledge of dangerous winds, rain, or snow can help save property, crops, and even lives. Fortunately, space science has provided meteorologists with a reliable and accurate tool for predicting the weather: the weather satellite.

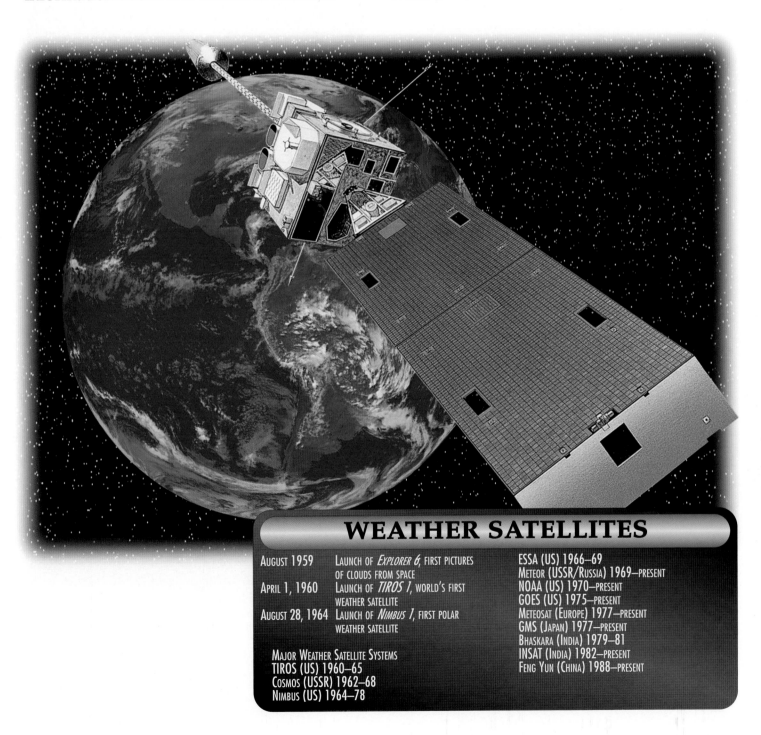

WEATHER SATELLITES

August 1959	Launch of *Explorer 6*, first pictures of clouds from space	ESSA (US) 1966–69
April 1, 1960	Launch of *TIROS 1*, world's first weather satellite	Meteor (USSR/Russia) 1969–present
August 28, 1964	Launch of *Nimbus 1*, first polar weather satellite	NOAA (US) 1970–present

GOES (US) 1975–present
Meteosat (Europe) 1977–present
GMS (Japan) 1977–present
Bhaskara (India) 1979–81
INSAT (India) 1982–present
Feng Yun (China) 1988–present

Major Weather Satellite Systems
TIROS (US) 1960–65
Cosmos (USSR) 1962–68
Nimbus (US) 1964–78

EYE ON THE STORM

The introduction of weather satellites, combined with the use of other advanced equipment such as supercomputers, greatly improved the accuracy of weather forecasts. At any one time, there are no fewer than a dozen different operational weather satellites from half a dozen countries orbiting the Earth. The images and other data from these satellites provide weather forecasters with details of storm systems, weather fronts, cloud formations, winds, rainfall, fog, ice, and snow.

The United States was the first country to test the idea of beaming pictures of clouds back from an orbiting satellite. In August 1959, *Explorer 6* radioed the first experimental photos of cloud cover from space. Eight months later, the world's first operational weather satellite, the Television and Infrared Observation Satellite (TIROS), went into orbit. Altogether, ten TIROS-class satellites were launched in the early 1960s, broadcasting almost 650,000 images.

Other countries around the world soon began launching meteorological satellites, with the Soviet Union launching its first in 1962. The European Space Agency's first came in 1977, and

China launched its first in 1988. More than two hundred different weather satellites have now been launched into Earth orbit. These include over sixty sent aloft by the United States. Today, more than 120 countries around the world receive most or all of their weather pictures from US satellites.

VERSATILITY

As weather satellite designers and engineers gained more experience of the new technology, the designs and functions of weather satellites became increasingly sophisticated. In addition to sending back photographs of clouds and weather systems, weather satellites began recording atmospheric and ocean temperatures at various altitudes and depths, and estimating rainfall.

Today's meteorological satellites can pinpoint weather formations with a high degree of accuracy. They can photograph clouds at night using infrared cameras, and take pictures in several different frequencies of light simultaneously. And to peer inside and through the clouds, some weather satellites use instruments that detect the microwave energy given off by the Earth and atmosphere. These instruments can scan cloud

formations to detect hailstorms and tornadoes, and can give as much as twenty-five minutes warning before a tornado strikes. In addition, they provide data about surface wind speeds over the oceans, ground moisture, rainfall, sea ice packs, and snow cover.

Weather satellites also produce other forms of useful

information about the Earth— for instance, by mapping the world's ocean currents, or by capturing infrared images of the Earth's surface that scientists can use to study land usage and assess crop health. Some of them can even listen for distress signals from ships at sea and downed aircraft.

A NEW ERA

THE AGE OF SPACE-BASED WEATHER FORECASTING BEGAN ON APRIL 1, 1960, WITH THE LAUNCH OF THE TELEVISION AND INFRARED OBSERVATION SATELLITE (TIROS). HARRY WEXLER, DIRECTOR OF RESEARCH FOR THE US GOVERNMENT WEATHER BUREAU, HAD SUGGESTED THAT CAMERAS IN SPACE WOULD BE ABLE TO SEE THE EARTH'S CLOUD PATTERNS, AND TIROS PROVED HIM RIGHT. THOUGH THE 270-POUND (122 KG) SATELLITE OPERATED FOR ONLY 89 DAYS, IT RADIOED BACK 22,952 PHOTOGRAPHS OF CLOUD COVER FROM ITS 450-MILE (725 KM)- HIGH ORBIT, FOREVER CHANGING THE SCIENCE OF WEATHER FORECASTING.

HARD EVIDENCE

ORBITS
Weather satellites are launched into either polar orbits or geosynchronous orbits. Those in polar orbits usually fly at altitudes of about 450–900 miles (725–1,500 km), crossing over the north and south polar regions in each orbit. They take very detailed close-up pictures as the Earth rotates below, but only cross over any one spot on the Earth once per day. Geosynchronous satellites orbit at 22,500 miles (36,200 km) and stay in the same position over the Earth all the time. This allows them to take continuous pictures of the area below them and track the motions of weather fronts and storm systems as they occur.

WATCHING THE WEATHER

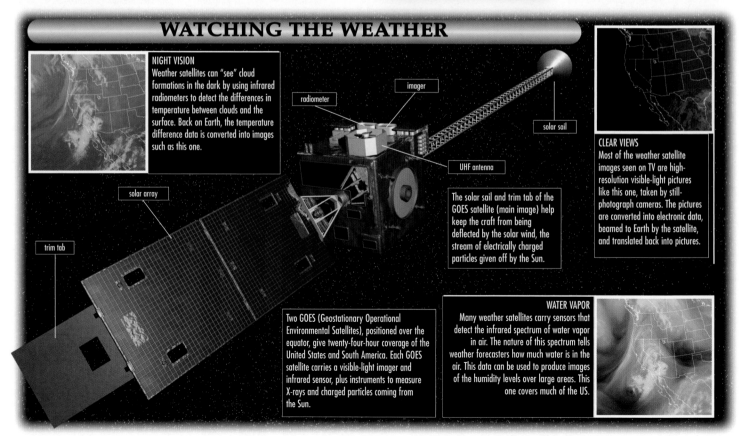

NIGHT VISION
Weather satellites can "see" cloud formations in the dark by using infrared radiometers to detect the differences in temperature between clouds and the surface. Back on Earth, the temperature difference data is converted into images such as this one.

radiometer

imager

solar sail

solar array

UHF antenna

CLEAR VIEWS
Most of the weather satellite images seen on TV are high-resolution visible-light pictures like this one, taken by still-photograph cameras. The pictures are converted into electronic data, beamed to Earth by the satellite, and translated back into pictures.

trim tab

The solar sail and trim tab of the GOES satellite (main image) help keep the craft from being deflected by the solar wind, the stream of electrically charged particles given off by the Sun.

Two GOES (Geostationary Operational Environmental Satellites), positioned over the equator, give twenty-four-hour coverage of the United States and South America. Each GOES satellite carries a visible-light imager and infrared sensor, plus instruments to measure X-rays and charged particles coming from the Sun.

WATER VAPOR
Many weather satellites carry sensors that detect the infrared spectrum of water vapor in air. The nature of this spectrum tells weather forecasters how much water is in the air. This data can be used to produce images of the humidity levels over large areas. This one covers much of the US.

X-RAY
SATELLITES

In 1962, as the US was hitting its stride in the Space Race, NASA sent up a small suborbital rocket to detect X-rays in space. Once above the atmosphere, which absorbs X-rays and therefore clouds data, the detector instantly recorded an abundance of these high-energy, short-wavelength rays, and astronomers realized they had found a new "window" through which to observe the universe. Since then, dozens of satellites have analyzed X-rays from hundreds of stars and galaxies—and revealed a complex X-ray "zoo" that includes some of the weirdest objects ever seen in the universe.

X-RAY SATELLITE LAUNCHES

1962	AEROBEE sounding rocket detects first cosmic source of X-rays	1991	*YOHKOH* ("SUNBEAM") X-ray solar observation satellite
1970	first X-ray satellite, *UHURU*	1993	Array of Low-Energy X-Ray Imaging Sensors (ALEXIS)
1974	*ARIEL 5* X-ray satellite	1995	Rossi X-Ray Timing Explorer (RXTE)
1978	Einstein Observatory (HEAO-2) launched, with X-ray telescope	1996	Satellite for X-Ray Astronomy (BeppoSAX)
1983	European X-Ray Observatory Satellite (EXOSAT)	1999	Chandra and XMM
1990	*Röntgen Satellite* (ROSAT)	2005	*ASTRO-E2* (*Suzaku*)

X-RAY HUNTERS

By 1970, rocket-borne experiments had identified over thirty X-ray sources in our own galaxy, and several more beyond it. But the exact nature of these sources was hard to pin down, because scientists could not actually see them.

A new window on the universe opened with the first satellite devoted to X-ray astronomy. This was one of the Explorer series of satellites, *Explorer 42*, originally called *Small Astronomical Satellite 1* (*SAS-1*) but later renamed *Uhuru*. Launched in 1970, it carried a simple X-ray detector and could measure the strength of X-rays and pinpoint the direction from which they were coming. *Uhuru* spent three years scanning the sky and recorded 160 X-ray sources. Its data revealed that most of the brightest sources were clustered along the plane of the galaxy, toward its center, and intriguingly, many X-ray sources were variable. One, named Centaurus X-3, pulsed on and off every 4.84 seconds on a 2.1-day cycle. What could the mysterious object be? What made the X-rays? And why the regular, rapid pulse?

Gradually, a theory emerged. A pulsing X-ray source could only be a neutron star—a small but super-dense object—that was sucking in gas from a neighboring star. This gas was being heated to millions of degrees and releasing vast amounts of X-ray energy. The rotation of the neutron star caused the pulsation of the X-rays. To study these extraordinary objects, astronomers needed details that *Uhuru* could not provide.

X-RAY IMAGING

The success of *Uhuru* encouraged the US, the USSR, and several European countries to launch many more satellites carrying X-ray detectors. But what astronomers really wanted was a telescope that could "see" X-rays, using carefully shaped mirrors placed almost parallel to the incoming rays to focus them onto detector instruments. This instrument would produce X-ray images instead of the visible-light images produced by ordinary telescopes.

A simple imaging X-ray telescope had been launched on a small rocket in 1965, and it produced crude images of hot spots in the Sun's upper atmosphere. Much better X-ray

images of the Sun were produced by the first large focusing X-ray telescope, the NASA Apollo Telescope Mount (ATM) that was flown aboard the Skylab orbiting laboratory in the early 1970s.

The experience gained during the design, construction, and use of the ATM was put to good use in the development of the first large mirror-based X-ray telescope. This satellite-based telescope, NASA's High Energy Astrophysical Observatory 2 (HEAO-2), was launched in 1978, and because that year was the centennial of physicist Albert Einstein's birth, *HEAO-2* was renamed the Einstein Observatory. It offered a one-thousand-fold increase in sensitivity compared with earlier

instruments, and by 1979, its seven thousand images had revealed thousands of new X-ray sources, in our own galaxy and in others.

The Einstein Observatory vastly extended the new field of study and discovered many X-ray sources, some of which can also be

seen with optical and radio telescopes. More than two decades later, X-ray satellites, including the Chandra and XMM orbiting X-ray telescopes, continue to add to our understanding of the galaxy and the history of its stars.

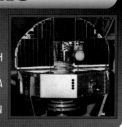

COSMIC RAYS

THE FIRST SATELLITE TO DETECT COSMIC X-RAYS, RATHER THAN X-RAYS FROM THE SUN, WAS ACTUALLY A SOLAR OBSERVATION SATELLITE (RIGHT). THE *THIRD ORBITING SOLAR OBSERVATORY* (*OSO-3*) WAS LAUNCHED INTO EARTH ORBIT ON MARCH 8, 1967, AND CARRIED INSTRUMENTS FOR DETECTING GAMMA RAYS AND X-RAYS. IT TRAVELED IN A NEARLY CIRCULAR ORBIT ABOUT 340 MILES (550 KM) ABOVE THE EARTH, AND MADE ITS FINAL DATA TRANSMISSION ON NOVEMBER 10, 1982.

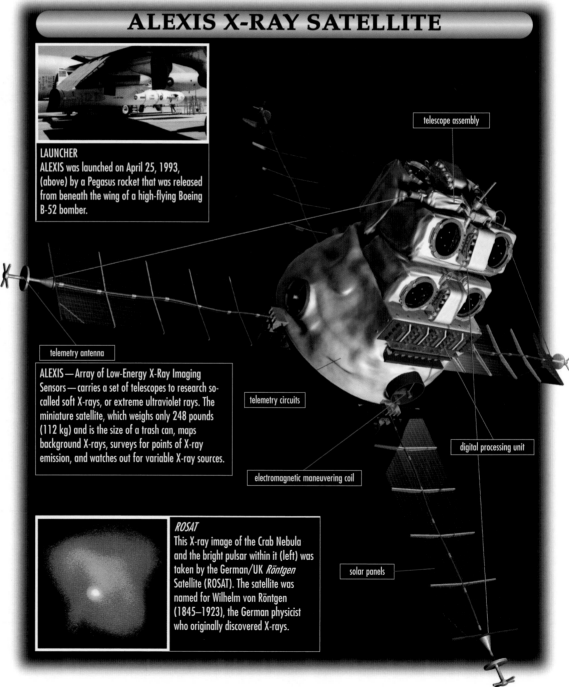

ALEXIS X-RAY SATELLITE

telescope assembly

LAUNCHER
ALEXIS was launched on April 25, 1993, (above) by a Pegasus rocket that was released from beneath the wing of a high-flying Boeing B-52 bomber.

telemetry antenna

ALEXIS—Array of Low-Energy X-Ray Imaging Sensors—carries a set of telescopes to research so-called soft X-rays, or extreme ultraviolet rays. The miniature satellite, which weighs only 248 pounds (112 kg) and is the size of a trash can, maps background X-rays, surveys for points of X-ray emission, and watches out for variable X-ray sources.

telemetry circuits

digital processing unit

electromagnetic maneuvering coil

solar panels

ROSAT
This X-ray image of the Crab Nebula and the bright pulsar within it (left) was taken by the German/UK *Röntgen* Satellite (ROSAT). The satellite was named for Wilhelm von Röntgen (1845–1923), the German physicist who originally discovered X-rays.

REMOTE SENSING

Today, dozens of remote sensing satellites scrutinize the entirety of the Earth's surface. With instruments and cameras that see farther into the spectrum than the human eye, they chart previously hidden geological features, record the shifting pattern of global land use, and uncover hidden archaeological sites. They also play a pivotal role in response to natural disasters and pollution control. Remote sensing provides a health check for the entire biosphere, and gives us new insights into climate change.

REMOTE SENSING SATELLITES

	Landsat 5	*Landsat 7*	*SPOT 3*	*Radarsat*	*Terra*
Operator	US	US	France	Canada	US
Launch Site	Vandenburg	Vandenburg	Kourou	Vandenburg	Vandenburg
Launch Vehicle	Delta	Delta	Ariane 4	Delta	Atlas 2AS
Orbital Inclination	98.2°	98.2°	98.7°	98.6°	98.2°
Mass	4,266 lb (1,935 kg)	4,332 lb (1,964 kg)	4,195 lb (1,900 kg)	5,969 lb (2,700 kg)	10,679 lb (4,843 kg)
Instruments	Multispectral scanner and thematic mapper	Enhanced thematic mapper	2 high-resolution cameras	Synthetic aperture radar	Multispectra imagers, radiation, and gas detectors

SCENES FROM SPACE

Remote sensing from space detects features invisible to ground-level observers and has transformed our knowledge of the Earth. Mining companies use remote sensing imagery to guide excavations. Farmers can accurately estimate seasonal crop yields. Before-and-after pictures of communities hit by floods or hurricanes help disaster relief efforts. Authorities identify tankers illegally dumping fuel at sea. And fast-food companies assess suburb growth to locate new restaurants.

Satellite-mounted cameras permit the simultaneous observation of large areas of the Earth's surface. Along with this wide perspective, they also allow a deeper view—into electromagnetic (EM) wavelengths beyond the range of human vision. EM energy from the Sun is variously scattered, reflected, or absorbed by terrestrial materials. Different materials reflect solar energy in different ways, some of which our eyes detect as the various colors of visible light. But light comprises only a tiny fraction of the entire EM spectrum. For instance, vegetation reflects with more intensity in infrared than it does in visible light, and its exact reflectivity provides a guide to its state of health.

Besides reflected infrared radiation, everything with a temperature of above absolute zero gives out thermal infrared radiation. By measuring this radiation, researchers can learn a material's physical characteristics and temperature. Remote sensing cameras typically image several different visible and infrared EM bands at once. These correspond to the reflected or emitted energy of specific materials—loose sand, say, or cultivated soil, vegetation, water, or different mineral types.

As well as these "passive" methods, satellites can also use "active" sensing. Satellite-mounted Synthetic Aperture Radar (SAR), for example, beams radio waves to the ground and records their reflection. SAR can penetrate cloud cover, vegetation, or even layers of surface soil.

Remote sensing spacecraft were developed from early weather satellites, which had simple onboard infrared cameras to image cloud formations by night. The first dedicated remote sensing satellite was *Landsat 1*, equipped with a multispectral camera that transmitted digital data, launched in 1972. There have been Landsat satellites in orbit ever since. *Landsat 7* was launched by NASA in April 1999. Its predecessor, *Landsat 5*, is still in service, although it is now operated by the commercial company Space Imaging EOSAT. The satellites are able to photograph almost the whole Earth every sixteen days.

In turn, the Landsats have inspired various foreign equivalents, such as the French SPOT series, the Russian *Meteor-Priroda*, and counterparts from Europe, Canada, China, and Japan. And along with the National Oceanographic and Atmospheric Administration, NASA operates remote sensing satellites to monitor the Earth's oceans and poles.

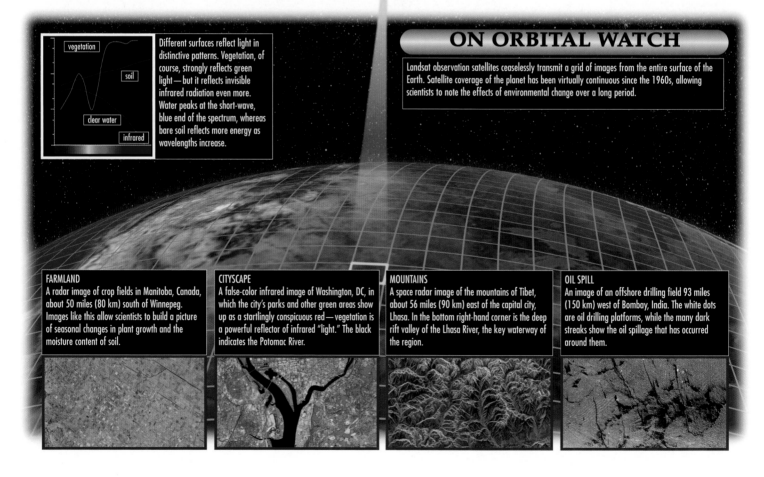

Different surfaces reflect light in distinctive patterns. Vegetation, of course, strongly reflects green light—but it reflects invisible infrared radiation even more. Water peaks at the short-wave, blue end of the spectrum, whereas bare soil reflects more energy as wavelengths increase.

vegetation

soil

clear water

infrared

ON ORBITAL WATCH

Landsat observation satellites ceaselessly transmit a grid of images from the entire surface of the Earth. Satellite coverage of the planet has been virtually continuous since the 1960s, allowing scientists to note the effects of environmental change over a long period.

FARMLAND
A radar image of crop fields in Manitoba, Canada, about 50 miles (80 km) south of Winnepeg. Images like this allow scientists to build a picture of seasonal changes in plant growth and the moisture content of soil.

CITYSCAPE
A false-color infrared image of Washington, DC, in which the city's parks and other green areas show up as a startlingly conspicuous red—vegetation is a powerful reflector of infrared "light." The black indicates the Potomac River.

MOUNTAINS
A space radar image of the mountains of Tibet, about 56 miles (90 km) east of the capital city, Lhasa. In the bottom right-hand corner is the deep rift valley of the Lhasa River, the key waterway of the region.

OIL SPILL
An image of an offshore drilling field 93 miles (150 km) west of Bombay, India. The white dots are oil drilling platforms, while the many dark streaks show the oil spillage that has occurred around them.

SATELLITES AND MOBILE PHONES

The cellular telephone system has freed phone users all over the world from the restrictions of hardwired landlines and given them the ability to make calls on the move—plus a whole lot more, but the system has its limitations. To get a connection, you have to be within range of a base station. If your phone isn't compatible with the systems in other countries, you won't be able to use it abroad. These restrictions would vanish if the new generation of mobile phones could link directly to satellites. However, this poses some impressive technical challenges which have yet to be overcome.

AIRBORNE ALTERNATIVE

A Proteus HALE unmanned aircraft could circle for hours at 60,000 feet (18,000 m), with its large antenna relaying phone signals as effectively as an expensive satellite.

GOING GLOBAL

Iridium was to be the first of the new systems to become operational. Originally intended to use seventy-seven satellites, this was amended to sixty-six, with eleven in each of six separate orbits. The satellites would travel at a height of 485 miles (780 km) and take less than two hours to orbit the Earth. An Iridium satellite's signal coverage would cover an area on the ground about the size of the eastern US. This area is divided up into forty-eight overlapping zones. A separate spotbeam of signals would serve each zone, measuring nearly 100 miles (160 km) across.

Calls from Iridium phones would be routed by the satellite. A call from one Iridium phone to another could be sent directly if both phones are covered by the same satellite. If one was farther away, the call would be cross-linked to another Iridium satellite that can "see" the other phone. If the call is to a non-Iridium phone, the message would be routed to an Iridium ground station, either directly or via a number of other Iridium satellites. From the ground station it would enter the ordinary telephone system and then proceed to its destination.

Calls to Iridium phones from other networks would be routed in the opposite direction. During the course of a conversation, the satellite handling the call would of course move across the sky and perhaps go "out of sight" of either person talking. If that happened, the system was set up to automatically transfer the call signal to another Iridium satellite in the same orbit or in a neighboring one. The other systems were to work in a broadly similar way.

SATELLITE CONSTELLATIONS

The Ellipso system was to deploy its satellites in two "sub-constellations" with Ellipso-Borealis covering the north of the Earth and Ellipso-Concordia covering the tropical and southern latitudes. Ellipso-Borealis was to have five satellites in each of two orbits; Ellipso-Concordia would have had six satellites in one orbit and four in the other.

Creating a useful handheld satellite receiver proved to be an immense technical challenge. Attaché-case sized units were possible, such as the Inmarsat unit, but mobile phone users have become accustomed to small, slim handsets and are not inclined to buy a large and bulky unit that does not offer many advantages over the existing ground-based cellphone system.

Thus Iridium and other satellite phone networks never quite came to be. It is likely that the concept will be revisited at some point in the future, however. In the meantime other technical innovations are entering the market. Landlines and satellites also could be joined by yet another new communications link: High Altitude Long Endurance (HALE).

HALE uses large airborne antenna to relay the signals of phones and ground stations. These antenna will be carried on HALE aircraft—airplanes or balloons—that will fly high over densely populated areas. Each aircraft will stay aloft for eighteen hours or more and may operate under remote control. Relief aircraft will take over at refueling time, so HALE will provide continuous service. HALE is not a space-based system, but it is based on the same concepts.

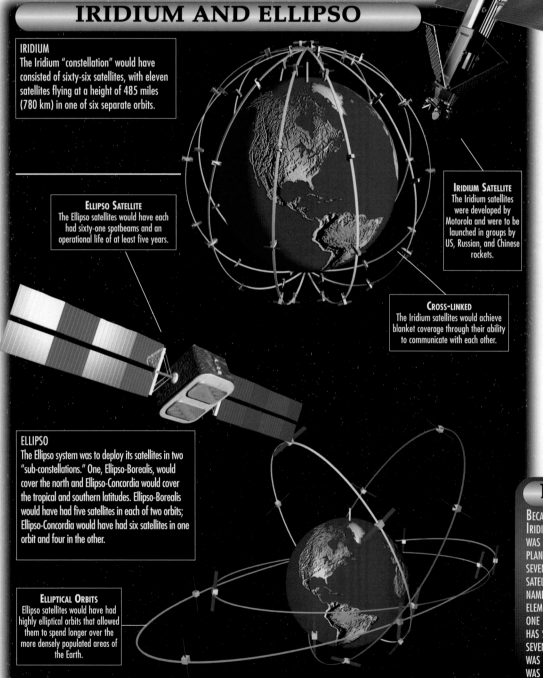

IRIDIUM AND ELLIPSO

IRIDIUM
The Iridium "constellation" would have consisted of sixty-six satellites, with eleven satellites flying at a height of 485 miles (780 km) in one of six separate orbits.

ELLIPSO SATELLITE
The Ellipso satellites would have each had sixty-one spotbeams and an operational life of at least five years.

IRIDIUM SATELLITE
The Iridium satellites were developed by Motorola and were to be launched in groups by US, Russian, and Chinese rockets.

CROSS-LINKED
The Iridium satellites would achieve blanket coverage through their ability to communicate with each other.

ELLIPSO
The Ellipso system was to deploy its satellites in two "sub-constellations." One, Ellipso-Borealis, would cover the north and Ellipso-Concordia would cover the tropical and southern latitudes. Ellipso-Borealis would have had five satellites in each of two orbits; Ellipso-Concordia would have had six satellites in one orbit and four in the other.

ELLIPTICAL ORBITS
Ellipso satellites would have had highly elliptical orbits that allowed them to spend longer over the more densely populated areas of the Earth.

ELEMENTARY

BECAUSE THE IRIDIUM SYSTEM WAS ORIGINALLY PLANNED TO HAVE SEVENTY-SEVEN SATELLITES, IT WAS NAMED FOR THE ELEMENT IRIDIUM, ONE ATOM WHICH HAS SEVENTY-SEVEN ELECTRONS ORBITING ITS NUCLEUS. THE SYSTEM WAS REDUCED TO JUST SIXTY-SIX SATELLITES, BUT IT WAS NOT RENAMED FOR DYSPROSIUM — THE ELEMENT THAT HAS SIXTY-SIX ELECTRONS PER ATOM.

HUBBLE
TELESCOPE

I n 1990, the Hubble Space Telescope (HST) was carried into Earth orbit by the Space Shuttle *Discovery*. Its original fifteen-year mission was to take a closer look at our solar system, the Milky Way, and other galaxies and to gaze back in time into the farthest reaches of the universe. Although there are larger telescopes based on Earth, the HST has the benefit of being above the atmosphere, enabling it to give us a much clearer view of the heavens—the pictures it has sent back have been truly stunning.

HUBBLE SPACE TELESCOPE

MASS	11.4 TONS (10.3 METRIC TONS)	ANGULAR RESOLUTION	0.1 ARC-SEC
LENGTH	43 FT (13 M)	POINTING ACCURACY	0.007 ARC-SEC FOR 24 HR
DIAMETER	14 FT (4.2 M)	MAGNITUDE RANGE	5 TO 29
PRIMARY MIRROR	8 FT (2.4 M)	ORBIT	380 MILES (611 KM)
SECONDARY MIRROR	1 FT (30 CM)	ORBITAL PERIOD	94 MIN
WAVELENGTH RANGE	110 NANOMETERS (UV) TO 1 MM (IR)	PLANNED LIFETIME	15 YR
		CURRENT LIFETIME	24 YR

WINDOW ON THE UNIVERSE

No matter how big you build an Earth-based telescope, it has one great drawback: the atmosphere absorbs and deflects incoming light, thereby degrading the view. The solution—putting a telescope into orbit—only became feasible with the development of the Space Shuttle, due to the size and sensitivity of the equipment involved. Even so, plans for a Large Space Telescope or LST (named Hubble in 1983) were already well under way by the time of the launch of the first shuttle, *Columbia*, in 1981.

GROUND CONTROL

The Hubble is roughly the size of a railroad car and built to fit inside the Shuttle's cargo bay. It occupies a low Earth orbit, circling at an altitude of just 320 miles (515 km). Attached to its "eyepiece" are two cameras—one that looks in great detail at a small area of space, and one that focuses on much larger areas or objects. Other instruments analyze the infrared waveband and characteristics of light.

Data from Hubble is relayed to White Sands, New Mexico, then on to Mission Control at the Goddard Space Flight Center near Washington, DC. Another link forwards the data to the Space Telescope Science Institute in Baltimore, Maryland. The HST costs an estimated $8 a second to use. Excluding the cost of shuttle launches, at least $10 billion has been spent on the Hubble to date.

HUBBLE SPACE TELESCOPE

1977 Hubble Space Telescope project approved. Budget estimated at $450 million — 85 percent to come from NASA and the rest from the European Space Agency. Launch date is set for 1983.
1979 Construction of Hubble begins. Launch is rescheduled for 1986.
1986 Launch of Hubble is postponed by the *Challenger* disaster. By now costs have already soared to $1.6 billion — three times the original budget.
April 24, 1990 Hubble is finally launched in the cargo bay of *Discovery*.
April 24, 1990 Hubble is deployed in low Earth orbit

(LEO).
May 20, 1990 The space telescope's "first light" — Hubble is turned toward the star cluster NGC 3532, but the image is out of focus, rendering the HST only marginally better than Earth-based telescopes.
December 5–9, 1993 Astronauts from *Endeavour* make the longest US spacewalk to date: 29 hours, 40 minutes.
December 18, 1993 Repairs proclaimed a success.
February 19, 1997 A second service mission adds two new instruments and effects running repairs.
1999 Service mission 3A installs new computer and replaces RSU (Rate Sensing Units)
2002 Service Mission 3B installs Advanced Camera (ACS) and replaces solar arrays
2004 Fourth service mission is canceled
2005 Hubble placed on 2-gyro operating mode, extending lifetime
2016 Hubble is still running.

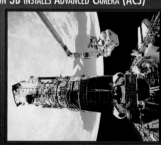

HOW BIG?
The Hubble can see out toward the farthest reaches of the universe, helping us to estimate how big it is, and also how old it is. Data from Hubble has helped scientists confirm that the universe will continue to expand instead of collapsing back in a "Big Crunch."

The HST was named after the astronomer Edwin Hubble (1889–1953), who discovered other galaxies and proved that they were expaning and speeding away from us. His work led to the development of the Big Bang theory.

LIFE SEARCH
The Hubble allows us to search for planets orbiting other stars, which no ground-based telescope can see. Where there are planets, there may also be life. Here, Hubble shows a new solar system beginning to form around the star Beta Pictoris.

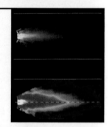

STAR DEATH
The Hubble telescope has brought us this spectacular picture of the Hourglass Nebula. The nebula is made up of the remnants of a dead star, puffed into space at the end of the star's life. By analyzing images like these, scientists gain new insights into the life cycle and evolution of stars.

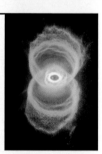

COMET WATCH
Although Hubble's pictures of other planets in the solar system cannot compare with those taken by flyby space probes, it does allow for regular and long-term observation. A prime example of the Hubble's value came when it showed the comet Shoemaker-Levy 9 as it crashed into Jupiter (right).

$1.6 BILLION BLUNDER

The Hubble's main mirror was ground from a $1 million blank by the US company Perkin Elmer, one of whose instruments was calibrated wrongly. The mistake should have been picked up by a prelaunch check, but Perkin Elmer was under pressure to deliver on time and on budget, so it was not spotted until the Hubble was in orbit. Dubbed "the $1.6 billion blunder" by the media, the fault was eventually corrected during a spacewalk by replacing one of the Hubble's instruments with a refocusing unit. The repair and servicing mission cost $800 million.

INSIDE HUBBLE

The Hubble Space Telescope (HST) is one of our single clearest windows on the universe, but it is neither the largest nor the farthest-seeing telescope ever built. What makes the billion dollar telescope so effective is its position—in near-circular orbit 330 miles (530 km) above the Earth. The images seen by terrestrial telescopes are smeared by atmospheric turbulence, dust, and light, so that fine detail is lost. But up in the vacuum of space, the HST's 94.5-inch (2.4 m) primary mirror is capable of resolving an image ten times better than even the best ground-based telescope.

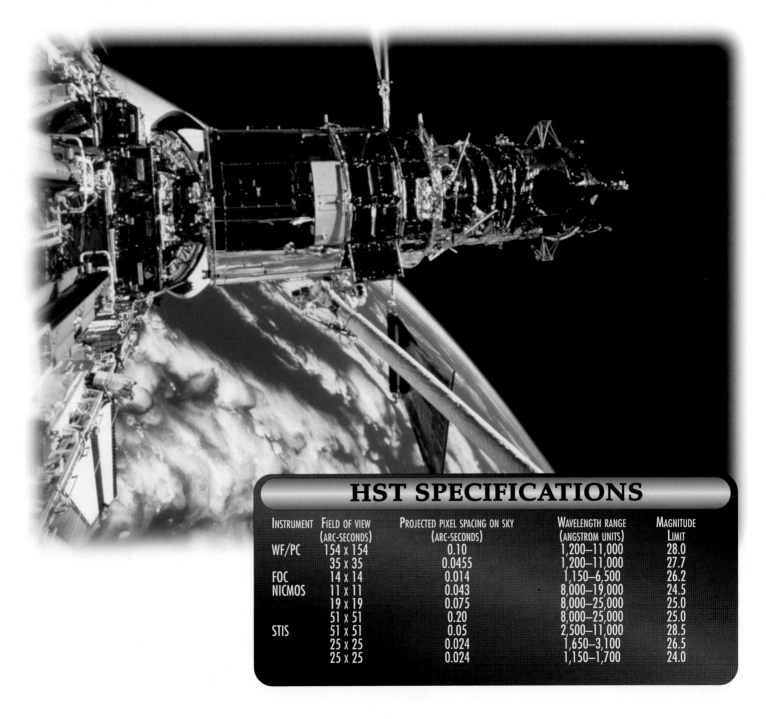

HST SPECIFICATIONS

Instrument	Field of view (arc-seconds)	Projected pixel spacing on sky (arc-seconds)	Wavelength range (angstrom units)	Magnitude Limit
WF/PC	154 x 154	0.10	1,200–11,000	28.0
	35 x 35	0.0455	1,200–11,000	27.7
FOC	14 x 14	0.014	1,150–6,500	26.2
NICMOS	11 x 11	0.043	8,000–19,000	24.5
	19 x 19	0.075	8,000–25,000	25.0
	51 x 51	0.20	8,000–25,000	25.0
STIS	51 x 51	0.05	2,500–11,000	28.5
	25 x 25	0.024	1,650–3,100	26.5
	25 x 25	0.024	1,150–1,700	24.0

FAR SIGHTED

The Hubble Space Telescope is essentially a telescope like any other, albeit one with 400,000 different parts and 26,000 miles (40,000 km) of electrical wiring, all designed to function in the unforgiving environment of outer space. The HST is an aluminum cylinder, 43.5 feet (13.25 m) long, fitted with a 94.5-inch (2.4 m) concave mirror at one end. This primary mirror reflects light back to a smaller, secondary mirror, which measures 12.5 inches (31.7 cm) in diameter. The secondary mirror redirects the reflected rays through a hole in the larger mirror into a rear bay, where separate cameras and instruments record and analyze the light. These currently include the Faint Object Camera (FOC), which is used to see extremely distant or dimly lit objects, and the Near Infrared Camera and Multi-Object Spectrometer (NICMOS). The latter is used to examine cool celestial objects and clouds that radiate infrared instead of visible light. Another piece of essential hardware is the Space Telescope Imaging Spectrograph (STIS)—this covers the ultraviolet, visible, and near-infrared wavelengths and can simultaneously divide light into its component colors at five-hundred separate points in a single image.

SPACE SENSORS

STIS can provide an instant chemical "fingerprint" of a planet's atmosphere, a dust cloud, or numerous stars within a galaxy. It gives information about the target's temperature, chemical composition, and motion. To steer the Hubble toward its astronomical targets, the instrument bay also contains three Fine Guidance Sensors (FGS). A star catalog listing fifteen million potential guide stars is used by the FGS as a reference. Another camera, known as the Wide Field/Planetary Camera (WF/PC), occupies a separate bay. It gathers light with a mirror mounted at 45 degrees, which intercepts part of the secondary mirror's beam. The WF/PC has taken many of the Hubble's most famous pictures, such as the famous image of the M16 Eagle Nebula. Like the Space Telescope's other instruments the WF/PC doesn't use photographic film—instead, it uses Charge Coupled Devices (CCDs) arranged in a distinctive "L" shape. CCDs are light-sensitive computer chips that are also found in consumer digital and video cameras. One of the WF/PC's four CCDs can be switched into Planetary Camera mode for a detailed view of a narrower area, such as the observation of a dust cloud on Mars. The CCDs are a hundred million times more sensitive than the human eye, but very vulnerable to damage—the HST cannot be pointed too close to the Sun or they will be burned out. As an extra safeguard, the Hubble has an aperture door. Should the spacecraft ever go out of control, it will shut automatically.

HUBBLE TECHNOLOGY

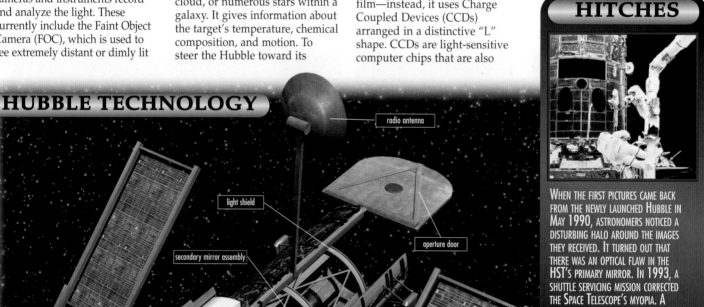

radio antenna

light shield

aperture door

secondary mirror assembly

primary mirror

aft shroud

guidance sensors

instrument module

solar panels

The Hubble Space Telescope is controlled from the NASA Goddard Space Flight Center in Maryland on the instructions of the Space Telescope Science Institute in Baltimore. It is moved by a system of four reaction wheels — their rotation transfers momentum to the spacecraft, moving the HST into position.

HARD EVIDENCE

ABOVE THE ATMOSPHERE
Air turbulence reduces the clarity of images received by ground-based telescopes. This random movement of air currents spreads a fuzzy patch of light around the center of stars, making them appear to twinkle. Astronomers favor observatories on mountain tops, where the skies are less polluted by artificial light and the air is thinner. High above the atmosphere, the Hubble is capable of resolving an image in space ten times more clearly than the best terrestrial telescope. Although the HST has made few fundamental new discoveries, it has given astronomers a much more detailed view of objects that were already well-known, such as the famous gas pillars of the M16 Eagle Nebula (above).

Gaseous Pillars - M16   HST · WFPC2

VENERA 1–3

In 1960, Venus was an enigma, its face veiled by clouds. And it was not only astronomers who were fascinated by this mysterious planet. The Soviet Union and the US were locked into Cold War rivalries and fears. Three years previous, the Soviets had shocked the Americans by placing the first satellite in orbit. Briefly, the US floundered, while the Soviets thrust ahead, seeking any project that would demonstrate their supremacy: more satellites, a man in orbit, and probes to the Moon and Mars—even to Venus.

FIRST SOVIET VENUS PROBE

FEBRUARY 4, 1961	*SPUTNIK 7*	FAILED IN EARTH ORBIT			EARTH ORBIT
FEBRUARY 12, 1961	*SPUTNIK 8*	VENUS FLYBY;	MARCH 27, 1964	*COSMOS 27*	FAILED IN EARTH ORBIT
	VENERA 1	COMMUNICATIONS FAILURE	APRIL 2, 1964	*ZOND 1*	VENUS FLYBY;
AUGUST 25, 1962	*SPUTNIK 23*	FAILED TO LEAVE EARTH			COMMUNICATIONS FAILURE
		ORBIT	NOVEMBER 12, 1965	*VENERA 2*	VENUS FLYBY;
SEPTEMBER 1, 1962	*SPUTNIK 24*	FAILED TO LEAVE EARTH			COMMUNICATIONS FAILURE
		ORBIT	NOVEMBER 16, 1965	*VENERA 3*	HIT VENUS;
SEPTEMBER 12, 1962	*SPUTNIK 25*	FAILED TO LEAVE EARTH			COMMUNICATIONS FAILURE
		ORBIT	NOVEMBER 23, 1965	*COSMOS 96*	FAILED IN EARTH ORBIT
FEBRUARY 19, 1964	*VENERA 1964A*	FAILED TO REACH EARTH			
		ORBIT			
FEBRUARY 19, 1964	*VENERA 1964B*	FAILED TO REACH			

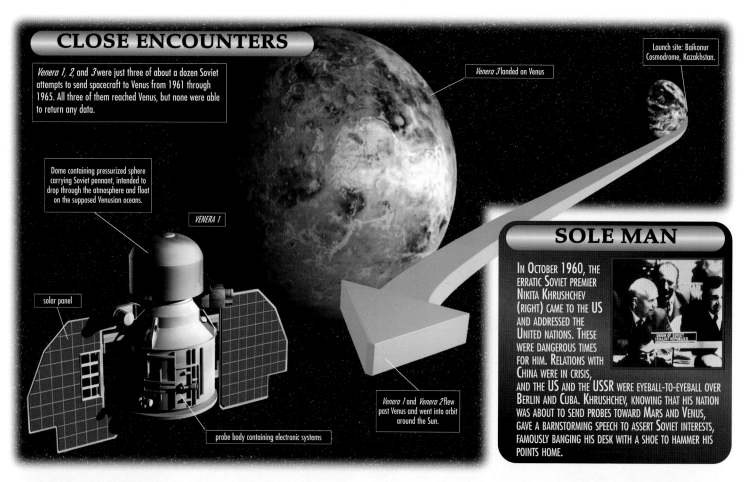

CLOSE ENCOUNTERS

Venera 1, 2, and *3* were just three of about a dozen Soviet attempts to send spacecraft to Venus from 1961 through 1965. All three of them reached Venus, but none were able to return any data.

Launch site: Baikonur Cosmodrome, Kazakhstan.

Venera 3 landed on Venus

Dome containing pressurized sphere carrying Soviet pennant, intended to drop through the atmosphere and float on the supposed Venusian oceans.

VENERA 1

solar panel

probe body containing electronic systems

Venera 1 and *Venera 2* flew past Venus and went into orbit around the Sun.

SOLE MAN

In October 1960, the erratic Soviet premier Nikita Khrushchev (right) came to the US and addressed the United Nations. These were dangerous times for him. Relations with China were in crisis, and the US and the USSR were eyeball-to-eyeball over Berlin and Cuba. Khrushchev, knowing that his nation was about to send probes toward Mars and Venus, gave a barnstorming speech to assert Soviet interests, famously banging his desk with a shoe to hammer his points home.

VOYAGES TO VENUS

In January 1961, when new US president John F. Kennedy announced that "the torch had been passed to a new generation," he took over a nation with no clear sense of its mission in space. Later that year, he would dictate an agenda that would take the US to the Moon. But currently the Soviets were reveling in firsts, including the first satellite in orbit and the first probe to photograph the Moon's dark side.

They were also aiming for the planets. Two attempts to launch Mars probes failed, but then Venus swung closer to the Earth, offering a four-month journey time—which was only half of that to Mars. On February 4, 1961, a three-stage rocket made it into orbit with a Venus probe in its fourth stage. But when the moment came to ignite the fourth stage and blast it toward Venus, nothing happened. The Soviets canceled the mission, which they called *Sputnik 7*, after one orbit, and explained the failure as a successful test of an Earth-orbiting platform from which a planetary probe could be launched.

A week later, *Sputnik 8* carried a second probe into orbit and sent it on its way to Venus. This time, all went well, and the Soviets code-named the probe *Venera 1*. Weighing half a ton, it had two solar panels and instruments to study cosmic radiation, micrometeorites, and charged particles. But seven days after launch, at a distance of 1.2 million miles (1.9m km), *Venera 1*'s communications failed and the course could not be altered. The mute probe eventually passed within 62,000 miles (100,000 km) of Venus, and on into solar orbit.

MINOR TRIUMPH

Three more failures in 1962 and four in 1964—which the Soviets tried to conceal—were crowned by modified success in November 1965. *Venera 2* was launched on November 12 and followed by *Venera 3* four days later. *Venera 2* was to make a close-up approach of Venus and take photographs. *Venera 3* was to enter the atmosphere, transmit data on temperature and pressure, and then release a descent capsule which would parachute down to the planet's surface.

On February 27, 1966, after more than three months of travel, *Venera 2* passed the planet at a distance of 15,000 miles (24,000 km), but again, just as the first pictures should have been sent, the communications system failed. *Venera 3*, after many mid-course corrections, was perfectly on target. On March 1, it hit Venus as planned but it, too, failed to transmit any information. The Soviets had to be content with a more minor triumph than they had originally hoped for: theirs was the first probe to reach another planet. But Venus would hold on to her secrets for a few more years.

MISSION DIARY: *VENERA 1–3*

FEBRUARY 4, 1961 FAILURE OF *SPUTNIK 7*, THE FIRST SOVIET ATTEMPT TO SEND A PROBE TO VENUS. FEBRUARY 12, 1961 *SPUTNIK 8*, PUT INTO ORBIT BY A MOLNIYA 8K78 ROCKET, SUCCEEDS IN LAUNCHING *VENERA 1* TOWARD VENUS FROM EARTH ORBIT. FEBRUARY 19, 1961 CONTACT WITH *VENERA 1* IS LOST. NOVEMBER 12, 1965 *VENERA 2* IS LAUNCHED FROM BAIKONUR BY A MOLNIYA 8K78M (R-7) ROCKET (ABOVE). NOVEMBER 16 *VENERA 3* LAUNCHED. NOVEMBER–DECEMBER SOME 13,000 MEASUREMENTS TAKEN TO ASSESS COURSES OF *VENERA 2* AND *3*. A TOTAL OF 26 COMMUNICATIONS SESSIONS INDICATE ALL IS WELL. DECEMBER 26 COURSE CORRECTION PLACES *VENERA 3* ON TARGET TO IMPACT VENUS (RIGHT) THREE MONTHS LATER. FEBRUARY 27, 1966 *VENERA 2* FLIES PAST VENUS AT 15,000 MILES (24,000 KM), BUT RETURNS NO DATA. MARCH 1 *VENERA 3* IMPACTS VENUS 250 MILES (400 KM) FROM CENTER OF VISIBLE FACE, BUT IT ALSO RETURNS NO DATA.

MARINER TO MARS

T he first close-up images of Mars, sent back by *Mariner 4* in 1965, shattered many illusions about the Red Planet. Until then, many people—including scientists—had supposed that Mars was an Earthlike planet, with water and perhaps a breathable atmosphere. There had even been speculation that lines on the surface, visible through telescopes, were canals built by the planet's inhabitants. But the information sent back by *Mariner 4* and its sister craft revealed that Mars is a dry, barren, uninhabited world.

MARINER MARS PROBES

Mariner 4			Dimensions	10 ft 10 in (3.2 m) tall, 19 ft ⅜ in (5.8 m) long (with solar panels extended)
Weight at launch	575 lb (261 kg)			
Dimensions	6 ft (1.8 m) tall, 22 ft (6.7 m) long (solar panels extended)		Power	450–500 watts from four panels of solar cells
Power	195 watts from four panels of solar cells		Data storage.	195 Mbits nonreusable tape (*Mariners 6 & 7*);
Data storage	Magnetic tape			51.22 Kbits reusable magnetic tape (*Mariner 9*)
Camera	Vidicon TV camera			
Telescope	30.5-millimeter focal length reflector		Cameras	Narrow- and wide-field vidicon TV cameras (508- and 52-mm focal length for *Mariners 6 & 7*, 50-mm for *Mariner 9*)
Mariner 6, 7, and *9*				
Weight at launch	910 lb (412 kg) (*Mariners 6 & 7*); 300 lb (136 kg) (*Mariner 9*)			

MARINER MISSIONS

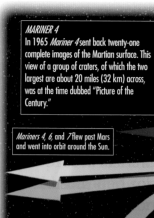

MARINER 4
In 1965 *Mariner 4* sent back twenty-one complete images of the Martian surface. This view of a group of craters, of which the two largest are about 20 miles (32 km) across, was at the time dubbed "Picture of the Century."

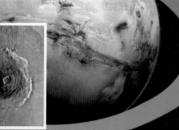

MARINER 7
Mariner 7 took this photograph of Mars as it approached the planet on August 8, 1969. The picture was snapped from a distance of 293,200 miles (470,000 km).

The launches of *Mariners 3* and *8* were unsuccessful.

Mariners 4, 6, and 7 flew past Mars and went into orbit around the Sun.

MARINER 9
One of the most famous images from *Mariner 9* is this view of Olympus Mons. The extinct volcano rises to a height of more than 78,000 feet (24,000 m), and its base is more than 300 miles (480 km) across.

Mariner 9 went into orbit around Mars.

DEEP SCAR

VALLES MARINERIS THE ENORMOUS RIFT VALLEY 2,450 MILES (4,000 KM) LONG AND UP TO FOUR MILES (6.5 KM) DEEP THAT SCARS THE SURFACE OF MARS, WAS NAMED FOR ITS DISCOVERER, *MARINER 9.*

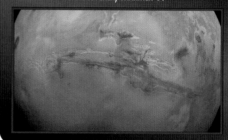

FIRST TO THE RED PLANET

NASA's Mariner missions to Mars contributed enormously to our knowledge of the planet, and the program was undeniably a great success despite the loss of two of the six probes shortly after they were launched. The first of these failures came on November 5, 1964, when *Mariner 3* was lost after the nose fairing of its Atlas Agena D launch vehicle failed to jettison and free the craft for its journey to the Red Planet. But three weeks later, its sister craft, *Mariner 4*, was launched successfully. When it swung past Mars at a distance of just 6,116 miles (9,842 km) on July 14, 1965, it sent back the first-ever TV images of the Martian surface.

When scientists received *Mariner 4*'s images and other data from Mars, they were stunned by what they saw. The TV images showed Mars to be a barren, cratered world, very different from the Earthlike planet that many had expected. As *Mariner 4* dipped behind the far side of Mars, the planet's atmosphere distorted its radio signals slightly. From this distortion, the atmospheric pressure was calculated to be between five to ten millibars—far too low to allow liquid water to exist on the surface. Furthermore, surface temperatures were estimated to be –148°F (-100°C).

The findings made depressing reading for those who had hoped that Mars harbored life.

The images from *Mariner 4* were limited and of poor quality, but Mars came into sharper focus when the more sophisticated *Mariner 6* and *7* flew by in 1969, a memorable year for NASA. Hot on the heels of the historic Apollo 11 Moon mission, *Mariner 6* and *7* swooped by Mars at a "grazing" distance of about 2,100 miles (3,370 km). Cameras attached to scanning platforms enabled each craft to collect sharp images of the Martian surface, and filters placed in front of the cameras meant that color photographs could be created. These showed the now-familiar rusty orange-red color of the planet's surface. But by chance, the cameras missed some of the most spectacular features of Mars' ancient terrain—its huge volcanoes, including the largest in the solar system, Olympus Mons.

MARNINER 8 AND 9

To achieve a global survey of Mars and find landing sites for future Viking craft, NASA needed a spacecraft in Martian orbit. *Mariner 8* and *9* were built to achieve this, but the initiative got off to a disastrous start when *Mariner 8* plunged into the Atlantic Ocean shortly after its launch in May 1971. *Mariner 9* was launched successfully, and on November 13, 1971, it became the first artificial satellite of Mars. But the first images showed absolutely nothing—for a planet-wide dust storm was at its height. When the storm finally subsided, *Mariner 9* made many important discoveries, including the Olympus Mons volcano and the 2,450-mile (4,000 km) -long Valles Marineris valley. The probe sent back a total of 7,329 images and was a fitting end to the Mariner missions.

STAR TRACK

CANOPUS

MARINER 4 WAS THE FIRST US SPACECRAFT TO USE THE BRIGHT STAR CANOPUS AS AN AID TO NAVIGATION. CANOPUS SIGHTINGS WERE USED EXTENSIVELY FOR ALTITUDE CONTROL AND NAVIGATION BY SUBSEQUENT INTERPLANETARY PROBES AND MANNED APOLLO MISSIONS.

MISSION DIARY: EXPLORING MARS

NOVEMBER 5, 1964 *MARINER 3* IS LOST IN AN ACCIDENT SHORTLY AFTER LAUNCH.
NOVEMBER 28, 1964 *MARINER 4* IS LAUNCHED SUCCESSFULLY FROM CAPE CANAVERAL, FLORIDA, ON AN ATLAS AGENA ROCKET.
JULY 14, 1965 *MARINER 4* PASSES WITHIN 6,100 MILES (9,800 KM) OF MARS AND SENDS BACK THE FIRST CLOSE-UP IMAGE OF THE PLANET.
OCTOBER 1, 1965 THE LAST TELEMETRY FROM *MARINER 4* IS RECEIVED WHEN THE SPACECRAFT IS 192 MILLION MILES

(308M KM) FROM EARTH.
FEBRUARY 24, 1969 *MARINER 6* IS LAUNCHED SUCCESSFULLY.
MARCH 27, 1969 *MARINER 7* IS LAUNCHED SUCCESSFULLY.
JULY 28, 1969 THE FIRST *MARINER 6* IMAGES ARE TRANSMITTED: THIRTY-THREE PICTURES OF THE FULL MARS GLOBE.
JULY 31, 1969 THE CLOSEST APPROACH OF *MARINER 6* ALSO MARKS THE END OF ITS MISSION.

AUGUST 5, 1969 *MARINER 7*'S CLOSEST APPROACH OCCURS WHEN THE CRAFT FLIES OVER THE MARTIAN SOUTH POLE AT A MINIMUM ALTITUDE OF 2,177 MILES (3,500 KM).
MAY 8, 1971 *MARINER 8* IS LOST AFTER LAUNCH.
MAY 30, 1971 *MARINER 9* IS LAUNCHED SUCCESSFULLY.
NOVEMBER 13, 1971 *MARINER 9* BECOMES THE FIRST ARTIFICIAL SATELLITE OF MARS WHEN IT ENTERS AN ELLIPTICAL ORBIT OF 1,050 MILES (1,689 KM) OF THE SURFACE.
OCTOBER 27, 1972 CONTACT WITH *MARINER 9* IS CUT, SIGNIFYING THE END OF THE MARINER MISSIONS.

VENERA 9 AND 10

Before the advent of space flight, Venus was an intriguing mystery to scientists. The Moon and Mars had been extensively studied by telescope for centuries, but the surface of Venus was hidden from view by impenetrable cloud cover, meaning that very little was known about it. In 1961, the Soviets began the Venera program—a long-term attempt to land a probe on the surface of Venus. After many attempts, some of which ended in success and some in failure, *Venera 9* and *10* sent back to Earth the first—long anticipated—black and white pictures of the surface of Venus in October 1975.

VENERA 9 AND 10

	VENERA 9	VENERA 10
LAUNCH DATE	JUNE 8, 1975	JUNE 14, 1975
DATE OF SEPARATION	OCTOBER 20, 1975	OCTOBER 23, 1975
DATE OF LANDING	OCTOBER 22, 1975	OCTOBER 25, 1975
LANDING TIME	5:13 A.M. GMT	5:17 A.M. GMT
LANDING SITE	32° S, 291° E	16° N, 291° E
DURATION OF SURFACE OPERATION	53 MINUTES	65 MINUTES

VENUS BOUND

By 1975, eight Venera spacecraft had left Earth orbit en route to Venus. The Venera series had proved highly successful, exposing many of the planet's mysteries for the first time. Two of the eight craft had descended into the atmosphere, sending back data describing a hostile environment with an atmospheric pressure ninety times that of Earth, surface temperatures over 900°F (480°C), and an atmosphere composed of 97 percent carbon dioxide.

For the next series of Venera, the Soviet Union developed more advanced craft, capable of returning pictures from the surface for the first time. The Soviets launched two new missions to Venus during the 1975 launch window. *Venera 9* lifted off on June 8, 1975, followed six days later by *Venera 10*. Once placed in orbit by a Proton booster, mission controllers gave them a final check before igniting the rocket stage to propel the spacecraft on their three-and-a-half month journey to explore Venus.

Two days before arriving at Venus, the lander and the orbiter separated to follow different trajectories. The lander was encased in an 8-foot (2.4 m) diameter spherical capsule which would provide protection during entry. The hermetically sealed sphere distributed the heat load and prevented the craft from imploding due to the immense atmospheric pressure. This protective heat shield was designed to survive temperatures up to 21,630°F (12,000°C). To give it even more protection from the fiery atmosphere, the lander was

1 Venera orbital station before research station separation.

2 After entering the atmosphere, the hemispherical covers of the research station separate.

3 Three main parachutes deploy at 40 miles (65 km) above the surface.

4 On landing, a shock-absorbing landing ring cushions the impact.

VENERA 9
The craft consisted of a cylinder with two solar panels and a parabolic antenna. A bell-shape unit holding the propulsion system was attached to the cylinder's base and the 8-foot (2.4 m) diameter sphere held the lander.

DESCENT INTO A HOT WORLD

SURFACE PHOTO
The *Venera 9* lander operated for fifty-three minutes, long enough to return this one image of the surface of Venus. Angular and weathered rocks, 11–15 inches (25–40 cm) across, dominate the landscape.

cooled with refrigerant before it began its descent.

SUCCESSFUL LANDING

Forty miles from the surface, the heat shield was discarded and parachutes were deployed to stabilize the lander and slow descent. At 31 miles (50 km) from the surface, the dense atmosphere allowed aerodynamic braking. A circular collar around the top of the craft generated enough drag to

slow the rate of descent. Final touchdown, seventy-five minutes after entering the atmosphere, was cushioned by a metallic shock-absorbing ring.

The *Venera 9* operated for fifty-three minutes before failure. Three days later, *Venera 10* touched down 1,364 miles (2,195 km) away and survived for sixty-five minutes. Surface data and video images collected by the probes were transmitted to the orbiter for later relay back to Earth.

The probes had also taken measurements of the composition of the atmosphere and structure of the clouds during descent.

The Venera orbiters relayed the data from the landers back to Earth and studied the planet's atmosphere. But the first photographs of Venus were the mission highlight. The images of the rocky landscape provided the first clues to our understanding of planetary evolution.

MISSION DIARY: *VENERA 9* AND *10*

JUNE 8, 1975 *VENERA 9* IS LAUNCHED INTO ORBIT BY PROTON ROCKET (RIGHT) FROM BAIKONUR COSMODROME IN KAZAKHSTAN.
AFTER ONE EARTH ORBIT *VENERA 9* ROCKET STAGE IGNITES.
JUNE 14 *VENERA 10* IS LAUNCHED INTO ORBIT FROM BAIKONUR COSMODROME.
AFTER ONE EARTH ORBIT *VENERA 10* ROCKET STAGE IGNITES.
OCTOBER 20 *VENERA 9* DESCENT CRAFT SEPARATES FROM ITS ORBITER.

OCTOBER 22 *VENERA 9* INSTRUMENT COMPARTMENT COOLED TO 14°F (-10°C).
DESCENT TO 78 MILES (125 KM) ABOVE SURFACE *VENERA 9* CAPSULE ENTERS THE VENUSIAN ATMOSPHERE (RIGHT) AT 6.6 MILES (10 KM) PER SECOND. THE TEMPERATURE IS 21,630°F (12,000°C). THE COVERS PROTECTING THE LANDER SEPARATE. AT A VELOCITY OF 820 FEET (250 M) PER SECOND, THE DROGUE PARACHUTE DEPLOYS.
40 MILES (65 KM) FROM THE SURFACE THREE MAIN PARACHUTES DEPLOY.
31 MILES (50 KM) FROM THE SURFACE PARACHUTES JETTISON; DRAG SLOWS CRAFT FURTHER.
OCTOBER 22, 5:13 A.M. GMT *VENERA 9* LANDS ON THE SURFACE WITH AN IMPACT VELOCITY OF 20–26 FEET (6–8 M) PER SECOND. THE TV CAMERA COVERS EJECT AND

CAMERA AND INSTRUMENTS SWITCH ON.
OCTOBER 22, 6:06 A.M. *VENERA 9* CEASES TO FUNCTION AFTER 53 MINUTES.
OCTOBER 23 *VENERA 10* DESCENT CRAFT SEPARATES FROM ITS ORBITER.
OCTOBER 25, 5:17 A.M. *VENERA 10* LANDS ON SURFACE OF VENUS. THE FIRST PHOTOS OF THE SURFACE (ABOVE) ARE RELAYED TO THE ORBITER.
6:22 A.M. *VENERA 10* CEASES TO FUNCTION AFTER 65 MINUTES.

VIKING
TO MARS

After a ten-month journey through interplanetary space, two US spacecraft reached orbit around Mars in the summer of 1976. *Vikings 1* and *2* were the most sophisticated robot probes yet built, and they had a mission to match their capabilities. While the orbiters mapped the Red Planet from high above its atmosphere, each one sent a Viking lander to make a soft touchdown on the surface. The probes beamed back the first images of the rock-strewn landscape, sniffed the Martian air and soil, took measurements of its chemical composition—and, most tantalizingly, searched for signs of life.

VIKING PROBE STATISTICS

VIKING 1	VIKING 2
LAUNCH AUGUST 20, 1975, KENNEDY SPACE CENTER	LAUNCH SEPTEMBER 9, 1975, KENNEDY SPACE CENTER
LAUNCH VEHICLE TITAN 3E-CENTAUR	LAUNCH VEHICLE TITAN 3E-CENTAUR
TOTAL MASS (UNFUELED) 3,247 POUNDS	TOTAL MASS (UNFUELED) 3,247 LB (1,473 KG)
MARS ORBIT INSERTION JUNE 19, 1976	MARS ORBIT INSERTION AUGUST 7, 1976
LANDING JULY 20, 1976, CHRYSE PLANITIA	LANDING SEPTEMBER 3, 1976, UTOPIA
ORBITER SHUTDOWN AUGUST 17, 1980	PLANITIA
LOSS OF CONTACT WITH LANDER NOVEMBER 13, 1982	ORBITER SHUTDOWN JULY 25, 1978
	LOSS OF CONTACT WITH LANDER APRIL 11, 1980

VIKING EXPLORERS

The Red Planet's first Earth visitor was a Soviet probe that landed in 1971. The probe transmitted TV pictures for twenty seconds and then went silent, possibly because of a radio relay failure—or perhaps as an unlucky result of the planet's most violent dust storm in decades. As that storm raged, the US Jet Propulsion Laboratory was steering Mars' first artificial satellite, *Mariner 9*, into orbit.

When the skies cleared, *Mariner 9* shot detailed TV pictures of the planet's volcanoes and valleys.

The data transmitted by *Mariner 9* proved vital in preparations for Viking's journey to Mars four years later. But Viking was a far more ambitious project than Mariner. The Viking team managed to launch two lander-orbiter combination craft within weeks of each other, bringing both Vikings into Martian orbit after a ten-month cruise halfway around the Sun.

The mission was one of the most complex ever attempted, as well as one of the most expensive uncrewed space projects to date, costing about a billion dollars. But Viking was worth every penny.

Both landers successfully separated from their orbiters and touched down on the planet's surface to begin examinations of Martian biology and sample the chemistry of this distant world. Neither lander found the hoped-for signs of life. Nevertheless, Viking was a great success. The orbiters sent back tens of thousands of images of Mars and its moons, Phobos and Deimos. They measured the structure and composition of the atmosphere, and detected water vapor. And the landers kept working for several years, providing valuable data on climate and seismology, as well as vivid panoramas of the dusty reddish landscape.

MISSION DIARY

NOVEMBER 15, 1968 PROJECT VIKING INITIATED (RIGHT) AS A JOINT VENTURE OF THE JET PROPULSION LABORATORY AND NASA'S LANGLEY RESEARCH CENTER. WORK SOON BEGINS ON THE LANDER'S PROTECTIVE AEROSHELL.
AUGUST 20, 1975 AT CAPE CANAVERAL, A TITAN ROCKET LAUNCHES *VIKING 1* ON ITS 62-MILLION-MILE (100M KM) VOYAGE TO MARS.
SEPTEMBER 9, 1975 *VIKING 2*

LAUNCHED.
JUNE 14, 1976 APPROACHING THE RED PLANET, *VIKING 1* CAMERAS COME TO LIFE, TAKING IMAGES OF THE GLOBE OF MARS (ABOVE).
JUNE 19 *VIKING 1* BRAKING MANEUVER PUTS THE SPACECRAFT INTO MARTIAN ORBIT.
JUNE 21 AFTER AN ADJUSTMENT TO ITS ORBIT, *VIKING 1* SCANS THE PLANET FOR A SUITABLE LANDING SITE.
JULY 20, 3:32 A.M. *VIKING 1* LANDER SEPARATES FROM THE ORBITER AND

BEGINS ITS DESCENT.
JULY 20, 6:53 A.M. *VIKING 1* LANDER TOUCHES DOWN IN CHRYSE PLANITIA; TWENTY-FIVE SECONDS LATER IT TRANSMITS A PICTURE OF ONE OF ITS OWN FOOTPADS ON FIRM, ROCKY GROUND (RIGHT).
AUGUST 7 *VIKING 2* ARRIVES IN MARTIAN ORBIT.
AUGUST 9 WITH THE HELP OF DATA FROM ITS TWIN, *VIKING 2* BEGINS THE SEARCH FOR A LANDING SITE.
SEPTEMBER 3, 5:37 P.M. *VIKING 2* LANDER SETTLES ON THE SURFACE THOUSANDS OF MILES FROM *VIKING 1*, AT UTOPIA PLANITIA.
JULY 25, 1978 *VIKING 2* ORBITER IS

POWERED DOWN AFTER A SERIES OF ALTITUDE CONTROL THRUSTER GAS LEAKS.
APRIL 11, 1980 *VIKING 2* LANDER TERMINATED AFTER BATTERY FAILURE.
AUGUST 17, 1980 CONTACT LOST WITH *VIKING 1* ORBITER.
NOVEMBER 13, 1982 PROJECT VIKING ENDS WITH LOSS OF SIGNAL FROM THE *VIKING 1* LANDER.

1 LOOKING FOR A LANDING SITE
On arrival in orbit, the *Viking 1* orbiter scans the planet for a suitable landing site. This painstaking investigation lasts for a month, until the region of Chryse Planitia (the "Plains of Gold") is finally chosen.

2 SEPARATION
On July 20, the *Viking 1* lander and its aeroshell receive the command to separate from the orbiter. The aeroshell slows the craft as it begins its descent and protects it from friction heating as it passes through the Martian atmosphere.

MARTIAN PANORAMA
Six minutes after touchdown, *Viking 1* transmits a panoramic view of the Martian surface. Suspended dust particles make the sky appear brighter than had been expected.

SOIL SAMPLES
Using a robotic arm, Viking takes samples of soil for use in four onboard chemical experiments that attempt to find signs of bacterial life. Results from both landers were inconclusive.

3 TOUCHDOWN
Four miles above the surface, the lander's 52-foot (16 m) diameter parachute opens. Seven seconds later the aeroshell is jettisoned; eight seconds after that the three lander legs are extended. At 1 mile (1.6 km), retrorockets fire and Viking makes a gentle touchdown on the surface of Mars.

MARS GLOBAL SURVEYOR

Mars Global Surveyor (MGS) is a surveyor satellite, weather satellite, and communications satellite all rolled into one. In circular polar orbit around Mars from March 1999 to the end of its extended career in 2006, its onboard cameras have taken thousands of high-resolution surface photos. It also returned daily temperature and atmospheric moisture data, lasting far longer than its planned two-year mission. Surveyor played a crucial role in Martian exploration and told scientists much about the Red Planet.

MARS GLOBAL SURVEYOR

MISSION PHASES		BEGIN MAPPING	APRIL 4, 1999
LAUNCH	NOVEMBER 7 1996	PAYLOAD	MARS ORBITER CAMERA (MOC)
MARS ARRIVAL	SEPTEMBER 12, 1997		MARS ORBITER LASER ALTIMETER (MOLA)
AEROBRAKING 1	NOVEMBER 7, 1997		THERMAL EMISSION SPECTROMETER PROJECT (TES)
SCIENCE	MARCH 27, 1998		MAGNETOMETER AND ELECTRON REFLECTOMETER
AEROBRAKING 2	SEPTEMBER 23, 1998		(MAG/ER)

MAPPING MISSION

Mars Global Surveyor (MGS) began its 466-million mile (750 million km) journey from Cape Canaveral Air Station on November 7, 1996. Once out of Earth orbit, the craft unfurled its twin solar panels, only for mission controllers to find that the latch on one of the panels had cracked, leaving the panel itself stuck at an angle. The panels were designed to provide power as well as to help the craft assume the proper orbit. Normally, this is accomplished by using the rocket engine to slow the craft. But the rocket used to launch MGS lacked the propellant to both lift the craft from Earth and slow it down once in Mars orbit. Instead, the plan was for Surveyor to initially assume a highly elliptical orbit. At the low point of this orbit, the craft would just skim the Martian atmosphere. Friction would slow the craft on each pass, until it finally assumed the correct orbit.

But engineers now worried that the stress of aerobraking could cause the damaged panel to break off entirely, causing further problems. Mission operators rescheduled the aerobraking procedure to place less stress on the damaged panel, revising the original four-month schedule to a longer, twelve-month schedule.

During the longer hiatuses from aerobraking, MGS was able to conduct scientific studies. During one such study, Surveyor's Magnetometer and Electron Reflectometer (MER) detected local "fossil" magnetic fields from Mars's oldest rocks.

On April 4, 1999, Surveyor finally attained mapping orbit and its original 687-day mapping mission finally began.

MAJOR DISCOVERIES

MGS's Mars Orbiter Laser Altimeter (MOLA) uses reflected laser beams to gather topographical details of the Martian surface. MOLA has turned up vast plains in the northern hemisphere of Mars, flatter than any of those yet found on Earth. These plains could be sheets of sediment left by evaporating oceans as the planet cooled over time, or possibly vast frozen lakes left covered in layers of dust.

The MGS's onboard Thermal Emission Spectrometer (TES) charts the temperature and chemical composition of both the Martian surface and atmosphere to provide a detailed mineral map of the entire planet. The most spectacular data are the 25,000 photographs taken by MGS. These reveal a dynamic world of winds and dust dunes. It is also a mysterious world, with numerous landforms scientists cannot explain. The two Martian poles appear completely different—the north is flat and pitted while the south has a series of holes and mesas. More mysterious still are numerous gullies that seem to have been caused by recent liquid water flows—which should be impossible according to conventional views of Martian geology.

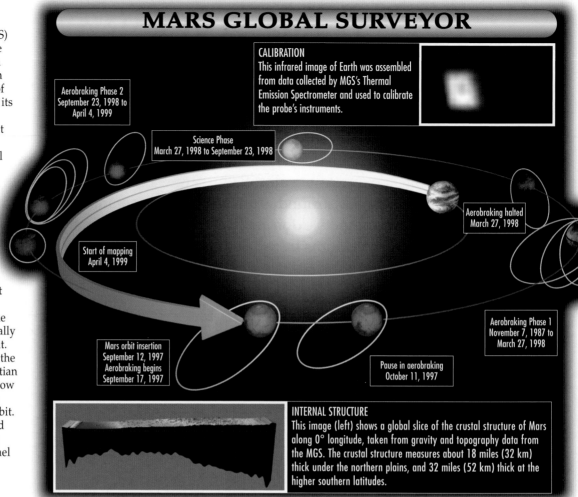

MARS GLOBAL SURVEYOR

CALIBRATION
This infrared image of Earth was assembled from data collected by MGS's Thermal Emission Spectrometer and used to calibrate the probe's instruments.

Aerobraking Phase 2
September 23, 1998 to
April 4, 1999

Science Phase
March 27, 1998 to September 23, 1998

Aerobraking halted
March 27, 1998

Start of mapping
April 4, 1999

Aerobraking Phase 1
November 7, 1987 to
March 27, 1998

Mars orbit insertion
September 12, 1997
Aerobraking begins
September 17, 1997

Pause in aerobraking
October 11, 1997

INTERNAL STRUCTURE
This image (left) shows a global slice of the crustal structure of Mars along 0° longitude, taken from gravity and topography data from the MGS. The crustal structure measures about 18 miles (32 km) thick under the northern plains, and 32 miles (52 km) thick at the higher southern latitudes.

MISSION DIARY: MARS GLOBAL SURVEYOR

NOVEMBER 7, 1996 MARS GLOBAL SURVEYOR (RIGHT, IN ASSEMBLY) IS LAUNCHED FROM CAPE CANAVERAL AIR STATION BY DELTA 7925 ROCKET (SECOND RIGHT).
SEPTEMBER 12, 1997 MGS ARRIVES AT MARS. A TWENTY-TWO-MINUTE FIRING OF MAIN ROCKET ENGINES PLACES THE SPACECRAFT IN AN ELLIPTICAL ORBIT.
SEPTEMBER 17, 1997 START OF AEROBRAKING. MGS PERFORMS A SERIES OF ORBIT CHANGES TO SKIM THE MARTIAN ATMOSPHERE, USING AIR RESISTANCE TO SLOW DOWN A TINY AMOUNT WITH EVERY ORBIT.
OCTOBER 11, 1997 PAUSE IN AEROBRAKING. TWO OF

SURVEYOR'S SOLAR PANELS HAD BENT SLIGHTLY UNDER PRESSURE — AEROBRAKING WAS HALTED TO ALLOW THEM TO RESUME POSITION.
NOVEMBER 7, 1997 RESUMPTION OF AEROBRAKING, AT A SLOWER PACE.
MARCH 27, 1998 AEROBRAKING IS HALTED TO ALLOW SURVEYOR TO DRIFT INTO THE PROPER POSITION WITH RESPECT TO THE SUN. THE HIATUS IS USED TO COLLECT SCIENTIFIC DATA.
SEPTEMBER 23, 1998 RESUMPTION OF AEROBRAKING TO SHRINK THE HIGH POINT OF SURVEYOR'S ORBIT DOWN TO 205 MILES (330 KM) FROM THE MARTIAN SURFACE

(VIEW OF MARS TAKEN MARCH 1999, RIGHT).
APRIL 4, 1999 SURVEYOR'S ORBIT REACHES A DISTANCE OF 205 MILES (330 KM) AND SCIENCE OPERATIONS BEGIN. MGS BEGINS MAPPING MARS AND INVESTIGATING SITES OF INTEREST.
2005 MGS MISSION CONTINUES RELAYING DATA TO EARTH.
NOVEMBER 2, 2006 EARTH RECEIVES ITS FINAL COMMUNICATION FROM MGS. FURTHER ATTEMPTS TO COMMUNICATE WITH THE SATELLITE ARE UNSUCCESSFUL.

PATHFINDER TO MARS

On July 4, 1997, an object that looked like a cluster of beachballs hit Mars's rusty surface, bounced, and came to rest in an ancient flood channel. The Mars Pathfinder mission had landed. The first spacecraft to visit Mars in twenty-one years, *Pathfinder* and its companion rover *Sojourner* spent almost three months probing the Red Planet. As planned, they beamed back reams of valuable new information about Martian geology and climate. Perhaps more importantly, as the pioneers of NASA's Discovery program, the two little probes inaugurated an exciting new era in space

PATHFINDER FACTS

LAUNCH VEHICLE	DELTA 2 7925 WITH PAM-D UPPER STAGE	CAMERA	STEREO; 140° FIELD OF VIEW
	PATHFINDER LANDER	*SOJOURNER* ROVER	
DIMENSIONS	TETRAHEDRON, 3 FT (0.9 M) TALL; WITH CAMERA, 5 FT (1.5 M) TALL	DIMENSIONS	2 FT (0.6 M) LONG, 1.5 FT (0.45 M) WIDE, 10 IN (0.25 M) HIGH
WEIGHT	2,062 LB (935 KG) AT LAUNCH; 793 LB (340 KG) ON MARS; 300 LB (136 KG) IN MARS GRAVITY	WEIGHT	22 LB (10 KG) ON MARS; 8.36 LB (3.79 KG) IN MARS GRAVITY
POWER	178 WATTS (DURING CRUISE); UP TO 850 WATTS (ON MARS)	MAXIMUM SPEED	2 FT (0.6 M) PER MINUTE

LOW BUDGET

The *Pathfinder* mission was the first in a new era of cost-conscious space exploration, a demonstration that NASA had opted for a "faster, better, cheaper" policy. Each spacecraft in the new Discovery program had to be designed, built, and launched within three years. It had to stay within a tight budget of around $150 million. Above all, it had to do the job.

Pathfinder's launch was routine, but its arrival on Mars was not. The probe slammed into the atmosphere at more than 16,500 mph (26,554 kmh). Its heat shield glowed as friction with Mars's thin air robbed it of its speed. At 1,000 miles per hour (1,600 kmh), a parachute opened. The probe still fell rapidly until, only eight seconds before impact, it fired braking rockets and inflated a cocoon of airbags. At 40 miles per hour (64 kmh), *Pathfinder* hit the rocky plain of Ares Vallis and bounced to a halt.

The airbag technique had never been tried before, but it worked flawlessly. *Pathfinder* emerged from its protective cocoon and, four hours later, released the Discovery program's next novelty: *Sojourner*, a tiny, six-wheeled autonomous rover. The first of its kind to see active interplanetary service, *Sojourner* was only 10 inches (25 cm) high; yet the rover contained an alpha proton X-ray spectrometer and a miniature processing lab that could analyze specimens of Martian rock and soil. As *Sojourner* toiled over its samples—each analysis required the rover to be stationary for ten hours—*Pathfinder* sent home streams of valuable data on surface weather conditions.

The mission blinked out on September 27, 1997, when the last successful transmission passed between Mars and Earth. NASA's new small-scale, elegant approach had been a triumph.

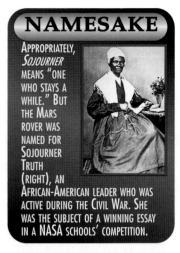

NAMESAKE

Appropriately, *Sojourner* means "one who stays a while." But the Mars rover was named for Sojourner Truth (right), an African-American leader who was active during the Civil War. She was the subject of a winning essay in a NASA schools' competition.

MISSION DIARY: MARS *PATHFINDER*

1994 Project planning begins.
June 1995 Descent systems — rockets plus air bags — are tested. *Sojourner* is developed on a simulated Martian landscape (right).
January 31, 1996 *Pathfinder* lander is teamed with *Sojourner* and test-fitted in the casing (second right) that will carry them to Mars.

August 14, 1996 Complete Mars *Pathfinder* probe arrives at Cape Canaveral to prepare for subsequent launch.
December 5, 1996 Mars *Pathfinder* is launched on a Delta 2 (left) from Cape Canaveral Pad 17B.

July 4, 1997 The probe lands only 13 miles (21 km) off target in the Ares Vallis region of Mars (right).
July 6, 1997 The *Sojourner* rover makes its first trip.
March 18, 1998 Mission concluded.

TOUCHDOWN ON MARS

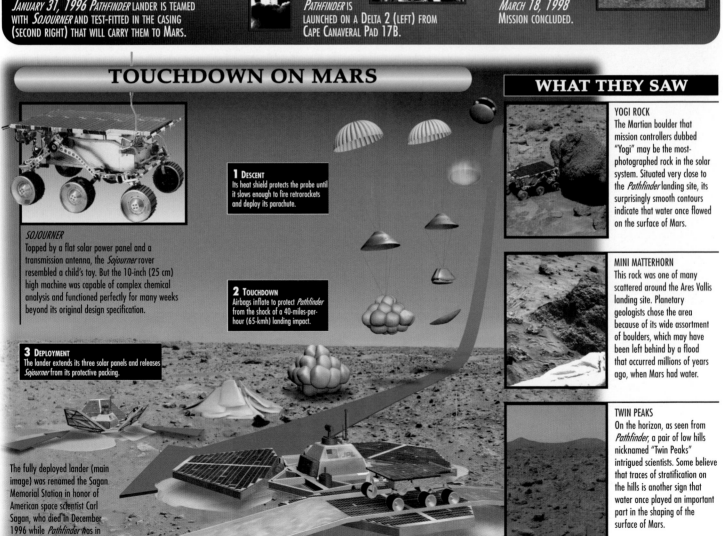

SOJOURNER
Topped by a flat solar power panel and a transmission antenna, the *Sojourner* rover resembled a child's toy. But the 10-inch (25 cm) high machine was capable of complex chemical analysis and functioned perfectly for many weeks beyond its original design specification.

1 Descent
Its heat shield protects the probe until it slows enough to fire retrorockets and deploy its parachute.

2 Touchdown
Airbags inflate to protect *Pathfinder* from the shock of a 40-miles-per-hour (65-kmh) landing impact.

3 Deployment
The lander extends its three solar panels and releases *Sojourner* from its protective packing.

The fully deployed lander (main image) was renamed the Sagan Memorial Station in honor of American space scientist Carl Sagan, who died in December 1996 while *Pathfinder* was in interplanetary space.

WHAT THEY SAW

YOGI ROCK
The Martian boulder that mission controllers dubbed "Yogi" may be the most-photographed rock in the solar system. Situated very close to the *Pathfinder* landing site, its surprisingly smooth contours indicate that water once flowed on the surface of Mars.

MINI MATTERHORN
This rock was one of many scattered around the Ares Vallis landing site. Planetary geologists chose the area because of its wide assortment of boulders, which may have been left behind by a flood that occurred millions of years ago, when Mars had water.

TWIN PEAKS
On the horizon, as seen from *Pathfinder*, a pair of low hills nicknamed "Twin Peaks" intrigued scientists. Some believe that traces of stratification on the hills is another sign that water once played an important part in the shaping of the surface of Mars.

MARS ROVERS:
OPPORTUNITY AND *SPIRIT*

I n a quest to discover once and for all whether water ever existed on Mars, two identical six-wheeled rover vehicles have followed the success of the much smaller Mars *Sojourner* by exploring further and for longer than any other mission to the Red Planet. Their data and successes have led to further exploration of the Red Planet.

MARS ROVER SPECS

MASS AT LAUNCH

ROVER	408 LB (185 KG)
LANDER	767 LB (348 KG)
BACKSHELL / PARACHUTE	742 LB (209 KG)
HEAT SHIELD	172 LB (78 KG)
CRUISE STAGE	425 LB (193 KG)
PROPELLANT	110 LB (50 KG)
TOTAL MASS	2,343 LB (1,063 KG)

REMOTE CONTROL

Launched on Delta II rockets, the Mars landers and rovers entered the Martian atmosphere inside protective "aeroshells." Each was slowed in the thin air by a parachute and Rocket Assisted Descent (RAD) motors that fire 30–50 feet (10–15 m) above the surface, bringing the vehicle to a dead stop. At the same time, a six-lobed airbag inflated and cushioned the impact of the craft striking the surface and subsequent bounces.

The two Rovers landed on opposite sides of Mars, with *Spirit* landing in the large shallow Gusev Crater near the south rim of the deeper Bonneville Crater. Its heat shield fell on the north rim and was spotted when *Spirit* drove up to the crater's edge. *Opportunity* landed on the Meridiani Planum, an area known to be rich in hematite, a material associated with hot springs or standing pools of water.

After several Martian days (sols), two-way communication was established and tested and the rovers were ready to explore Mars in more detail than had ever been possible before. To communicate with Earth, the rovers relay information by way of orbiting craft; 70 percent of the mission data is transmitted via the Mars Odyssey Orbiter and 30 percent by way of the Mars Global Surveyor.

Driving a vehicle by remote control 50 million miles (80 million km) from Earth requires caution. Several cameras are used to select a path, steer the rovers, and avoid close obstacles. The rovers are not designed for speed. On a hard, flat surface they could reach up to 2 inches (5 cm) per second, but were strictly limited by hazard avoidance software to ten-second runs, followed by twenty-second pauses to assess the terrain, giving an average speed of one-third of an inch (1 cm) per second. Records for distance driving in one day reached 722 feet (220 m) in March 2005. Driving over a surface and then reversing back allows the cameras to study the tracks and get an idea of the softness or otherwise of the terrain.

Each future move is discussed and planned in great detail before being commanded. A duplicate rover is tested on Earth

A photograph of the floor of Gusev Crater, taken by the first rover to land, *Spirit*. This is one of the first images beamed back to Earth from the rover shortly after it touched down, captured by the rover's panoramic camera.

DELTA LAUNCH

BOTH ROVERS WERE LAUNCHED ON DELTA II ROCKETS, ALTHOUGH THE ROVER B MISSION NEEDED A HEAVY VERSION OF THE ROCKET WITH MORE FUEL BECAUSE MARS AND EARTH HAD MOVED FARTHER APART IN THE MONTH SINCE THE FIRST LAUNCH.

on various simulated Martian surfaces, which are often tilted to angle equal to slopes faced by the actual rovers. Occasionally, softer than expected sand caused the rovers to become stuck for long periods. Scientists simulated this with various building and gardening materials and developed techniques for driving out of these "sand traps."

After exploring its immediate environment, *Spirit* then set off towards a feature dubbed the Columbia Hills. Each of the seven peaks is named for one of the astronauts lost in the 2003 *Columbia* disaster. The hills, rising to 300 feet (90 m) above the plain were estimated as 1 mile (1.6 km) distant, a drive that would take up to 160 sols if the rover lasted that long.

EXTENDED WARRANTY

Opportunity drove up to the stadium-sized Endurance Crater. After much debate it was decided to enter the crater as the possible science benefits outweighed the risk of not being able to drive out again. As it happened, *Opportunity* later became stuck in a sand trap for nearly five weeks but was successfully extracted.

Near its own heat shield, *Spirit* discovered an iron meteorite—the first meteorite discovered on another world.

Many other discoveries pointed to evidence of the former presence of water on Mars, the main scientific target of the

mission. These included: spherules; smile-shaped marks in rocks and ripple patterns on rock surfaces. Evidence of magnesium sulphates pointed to the evaporation of water in the distant past.

The rovers were able to observe the sky as well as the Earth, and photographed the Earth and stars from an unusual viewpoint. They also witnessed lunar eclipses where Mars's moons—Phobos and Deimos— passed in front of the Sun. A streak in the sky in one photo perplexed scientists for some time, but is now thought to have been the *Viking 2* orbiter, which is still circling Mars.

The rovers pleased NASA and the Jet Propulsion Laboratory by remaining in functional condition well past the "warranty" of their ninety-sol primary missions, which were completed in April 2004. From then on the crews could take greater risks than before. A software update allowed two hours "autonomous" driving each day after an hour of "blind" driving following a route preplanned on Earth. Autonomous driving, which in fact meant driving for 6 feet 6 inches (2 m) then pausing to look for obstacles, allowed the rovers to cover as much ground in just three sols as they had in seventy during early parts of the mission.

Dust accretion on the solar panels caused a reduction in available power from time to time and a partial loss of vision from the cameras, but strong winds later blew the dust clear, giving improved performance. While *Spirit* finally stopped communicating in 2010, to date *Opportunity* is still sending data back to Earth, over ten years since it landed on the surface of Mars.

MISSION DIARY

JUNE 10, 2003
ROVER A MISSION (*SPIRIT*) LAUNCHED.
JULY 7, 2003
ROVER B MISSION (*OPPORTUNITY*) LAUNCHED.
JANUARY 3, 2004
SPIRIT LANDS IN GUSEV CRATER.
JANUARY 24, 2004
OPPORTUNITY LANDS ON MERIDIANI PLANUM.

JUNE 8, 2004
OPPORTUNITY ENTERS ENDURANCE CRATER AND SPENDS FOLLOWING SIX MONTHS EXPLORING IT.
JUNE 11, 2004
SPIRIT REACHES COLUMBIA HILLS.
2010 *SPIRIT* CEASES TO FUNCTION.
2016 *OPPORTUNITY* CONTINUES ITS JOURNEY.

CURIOSITY

Launched on November 26, 2011, from Cape Canaveral as part of the Mars Science Laboratory mission, *Curiosity* began its initial two-year mission when it landed on August 6, 2012. *Curiosity* will continue the work of *Sojourner*—from NASA's earlier *Pathfinder* mission—*Opportunity*, and *Spirit*, by assessing the surface of Mars and analyzing its geology and climate. The rover will take these investigations further by evaluating the possibility of Mars ever having microbial life forms. The suspected presence of water on Mars has long made this an intriguing possibility. NASA intends to follow up the *Curiosity* rover with a further rover mission by 2020, with plans for human exploration in the future.

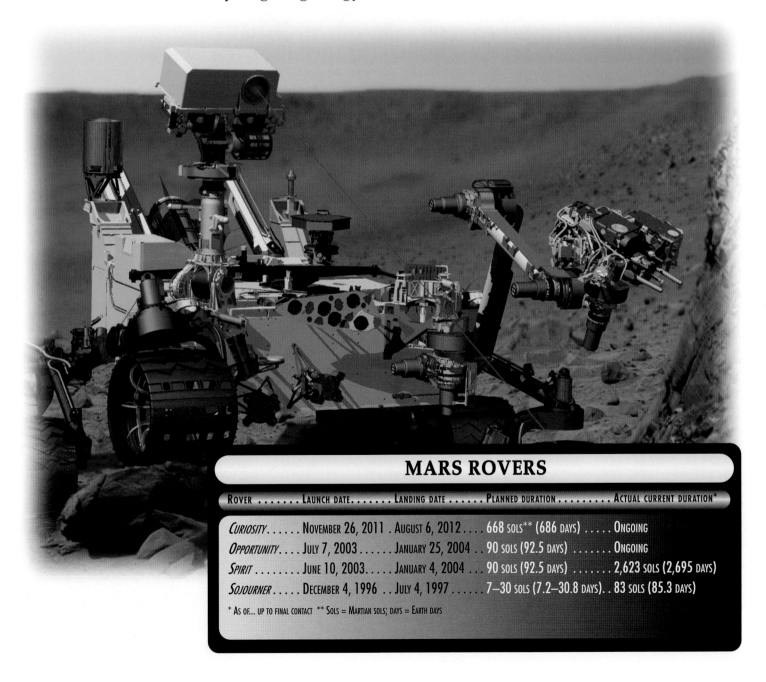

MARS ROVERS

ROVER	LAUNCH DATE	LANDING DATE	PLANNED DURATION	ACTUAL CURRENT DURATION*
CURIOSITY	NOVEMBER 26, 2011	AUGUST 6, 2012	668 SOLS** (686 DAYS)	ONGOING
OPPORTUNITY	JULY 7, 2003	JANUARY 25, 2004	90 SOLS (92.5 DAYS)	ONGOING
SPIRIT	JUNE 10, 2003	JANUARY 4, 2004	90 SOLS (92.5 DAYS)	2,623 SOLS (2,695 DAYS)
SOJOURNER	DECEMBER 4, 1996	JULY 4, 1997	7–30 SOLS (7.2–30.8 DAYS)	83 SOLS (85.3 DAYS)

* AS OF... UP TO FINAL CONTACT ** SOLS = MARTIAN SOLS; DAYS = EARTH DAYS

GETTING TO KNOW THE RED PLANET

The planned landing site for *Curiosity* was the Gale crater. With a diameter of 96 miles (154 km) and depth of approximately 3 miles (5 km), the crater has a dome in its center called Aeolis Mons, where *Curiosity* would start its investigations. The landing was successful, with the rover ending its journey only 1.5 miles (2.4 km) from its target, now known as the Bradbury Landing site (named after science fiction author Ray Bradbury). The crater was caused by an impact over three billion years ago. It was chosen for the landing site as the area is thought to have once contained water. With wind erosion exposing layers of sediment, *Curiosity* will analyze Martian geology going back billions of years—including the planet's evolution.

The site might also have once held water, a factor that could be key to any signs of life found on the Red Planet.

Curiosity was the first NASA Mars rover to land in an active state. On touchdown, it triggered explosives to free itself from the cables used for the 66-foot (20 m) descent stage. The spacecraft then crash landed at a prearranged site. The rover is also the first to collect samples of rock drilled from the surface of Mars.

Approximately twice the size and five times the weight of its predecessors *Opportunity* and *Spirit*, *Curiosity* shares the same basic design of six wheels, a suspension system designed to cope with the uneven surfaces of Mars, and mounted cameras to aid movement and record data and images, of which a huge amount has already been sent back to NASA's astronomers. The first NASA Mars rover, *Sojourner*, also shared this structure, although it was much smaller than the approximately 10-foot (3 m) length of *Curiosity*. The rover also differs in that it can also drill and gather samples of soil and rocks and even process these samples in its onboard test chambers, to identify and measure mineral levels and compositions. Its power generator means it can run for around two Earth years and cover more inaccessible terrain, while its camera is capable of taking extreme close-up images. Radiation measurements are also taken, which are vital for the future planning of any human exploration trips to Mars and their safe duration for the astronauts.

LIFE ON MARS?

Public support has been overwhelming, with the NASA website crashing when live streams of the first footage was aired on their website. One of the most enduringly popular topics searched for is whether or not *Curiosity* has been able to find any evidence of life on the Red Planet. So far, *Curiosity* has found evidence to support the theory that the environment on Mars was capable of supporting life in the past (with Mars now at a later stage in its possibly faster evolution than Earth). Whether *Curiosity* will be able to find anything that proves there was any actual life forms on Mars is as yet unknown, as well as what happened on the Red Planet to cause the end of any existing life. It may still be a long time before our curiosity is satisfied on this intriguing point, although a follow up NASA Mars rover mission is in the pipeline for 2020.

THE GALE CRATER
The trenches of the Gale Crater hold a mountain known as Aeolis Mons, known as Mount Sharp.

ROVING AROUND MARS

GETTING BIGGER
These tires give a representation of the difference in size of each lunar rover, ranging from *Sojourner* to *Curiosity*.

OPPORTUNITY AND SPIRIT
TThe main objectives of the combined Mars Exploration Rover mission are to analyze the geology and climate of Mars.

CURIOSITY
The main objectives of *Curiosity* are to determine whether Mars once held life and what its climate once looked like.

SOJOURNER
The main objectives of the Mars Pathfinder mission were to test run the equipment at lower costs than NASA's Viking missions.

WATER ON MARS
This image, taken by *Curiosity*, shows areas where the rover has found evidence of water existence on the Moon, usually found as ice or vapor. These areas are shown in color, with the brightest and reddest areas highlighting the presence of the greatest remains of water.

MAVEN

The Mars Atmosphere and Volatile Evolution (MAVEN) was launched by NASA on November 18, 2013, from Cape Canaveral, Florida. MAVEN entered orbit around Mars on September 22, 2014, following an areocentric elliptical orbit around the planet. MAVEN's aim is to discover more about the Martian upper atmosphere and climate, including how it was lost to space over time. The mission will last at least one year and data gleaned from MAVEN will be combined with surface data and measurements from the *Curiosity* Mars rover and aims to send back new data on the many mysteries still shrouding Mars.

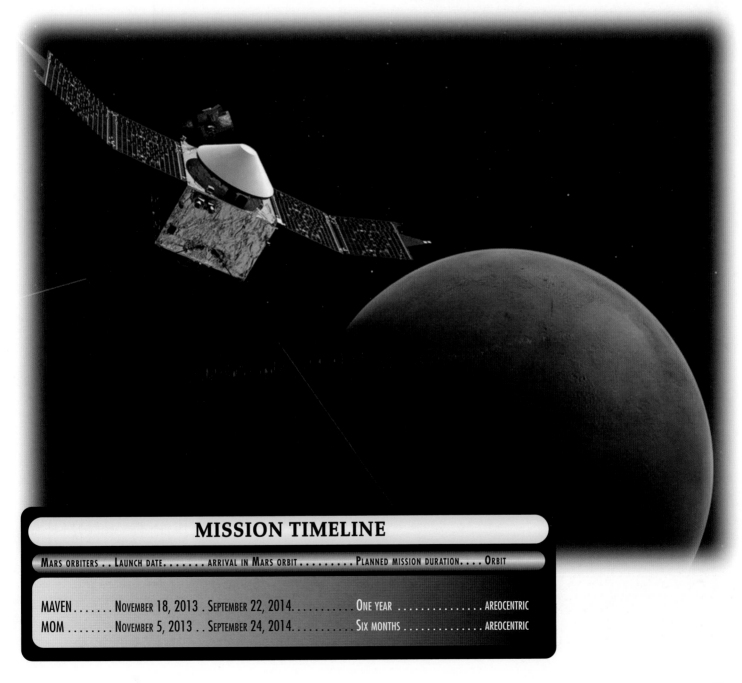

MISSION TIMELINE

Mars orbiters	Launch date	Arrival in Mars orbit	Planned mission duration	Orbit
MAVEN	November 18, 2013	September 22, 2014	One year	Areocentric
MOM	November 5, 2013	September 24, 2014	Six months	Areocentric

THE RACE IS ON

If its schedule goes to plan, MAVEN will beat MOM into orbit around Mars by a mere two days. The Mars Orbiter Mission is another orbiter, which was launched by the Indian Space Research Organisation on November 5, 2013. MOM marks the first ISRO interplanetary mission and will make it the fourth space agency to reach Mars. The purpose of the mission is to both explore the surface and atmosphere of Mars, and develop India's launch systems and spacecraft technology.

Both MAVEN and MOM will be key to discovering more about Mars's climate and how it changed so much. MAVEN will be focusing on Mars's upper atmosphere to find out why any water that might once have existed on Mars has now disappeared, perhaps escaping as gas through the diminishing atmosphere. MAVEN will be able to plot an orbit of 93 to 3,728 miles (150 to 6,000 km) above the planet's surface, including taking five "deep dips" down to just 93 miles (150 km) minimum altitude in order to take samples of the remaining upper atmosphere. The surface temperature of Mars is now too cold to support water as liquid, due to the planet's core cooling over millions of years. However, certain features of the surface of Mars suggest that water was present in large quantities, perhaps as rivers or lakes. There is also evidence of mineral deposits that require the existence of water, plus layers of sediment.

Additionally, the magnetic field around Mars has decayed over time, which has possibly resulted in the planet's low atmospheric pressure. This means that for the last few billion years, electrically charged solar winds of up to 1,000,000 miles per hour (1,609,000 kmh) would have begun to sweep away much of the atmosphere that helped keep the water on the planet's surface. MAVEN will be able to measure the rate by which atmospheric gases are lost, discovering more about Mars's history and atmospheric changes. In addition, data from *Curiosity* on the chemical composition of the surface of Mars will be used to measure current rates of atmosphere loss.

Built by Lockheed Martin Space Systems, MAVEN weighed 5,400 pounds (2,454 kg) at launch and stretches 37 feet (11 m) from wingtip to wingtip, with its core cubical module being 7.5 feet (2.3 m) high. It was rigorously tested to ensure it can survive the extreme temperatures and winds around Mars. The orbiter is equipped with a Particles and Field package, which measures solar wind and energy particles, as well as magnetic fields and ions. MAVEN's mission is currently estimated to last one Earth year.

STAYING ON SCHEDULE

After ten years of preparation and a budget of $650 million, government personnel strikes almost cost MAVEN its launch date, which would have meant missing the narrow launch window of twenty days. If missed, it would be twenty-six months until Mars moved back into the correct alignment with Earth, meaning that MOM would have beaten MAVEN into orbit by quite some time. The seventeen-day strikes—which took place only seven weeks before the launch date—were only resolved when emergency funding was released to allow the launch to go ahead as scheduled. It was also partly due to the effective team members being slightly ahead of schedule and being so eager to return to work and ensure the launch went ahead.

DISCOVERING MARS

THE RED PLANET
Mars has intrigued astronmers ever since it was discovered that its atmosphere could have once held life.

LAUNCH
This picturesque image shows MAVEN being successfully launched from Cape Canaveral. MAVEN remains on course for many future successes.

MARS NOW
This artist's interpretation shows the surface of Mars as it is today; dry, dusty, and waterless.

MARS THEN
Here Mars is shown awash with mountains and lakes, with a blue cloudy sky much like Earth's.

EXPLORING FURTHER

Exploration of the outer planets is a time-consuming business due to the great distances involved. The length of some missions has exceeded the careers of the scientists who devised and nurtured them. *Pioneer 10* passed Jupiter in December 1973, and in 1990 it became the first man-made object to leave the solar system. It was last heard from in 2003 when over 10.6 billion miles (17 billion km) from Earth. The *Huygens* probe touched down on Saturn's moon Titan in January 2005, making the farthest landing from Earth. The *Cassini* mothership continues to study Saturn, Titan, and Saturn's thirty-two other moons. Experiments are underway to use solar wind to power future spacecraft, with photons from the sun pushing against a sail made of Mylar or a similar thin, lightweight fabric. Such a craft would accelerate very slowly, but would eventually reach enormous velocities. For example, a future probe to the outer solar system could reach 60,000 miles per hour (100,000 kmh) in three years, enough to reach the dwarf planet Pluto in about half the time of a conventionally powered spacecraft.

PIONEER SOLAR
MISSIONS

Although the earliest US interplanetary probes lost the race to the Moon, they discovered something more interesting along the way: a torrent of charged particles emanating from the Sun. Instead of jockeying for a piece of lunar territory, the later Pioneer probes were sent into orbit around our nearest star. Weighing in at about 140 pounds (64 kg), these little explorers proved that interplanetary space—previously thought to be empty—is filled with powerful magnetic fields and a strong wind that blows from the Sun.

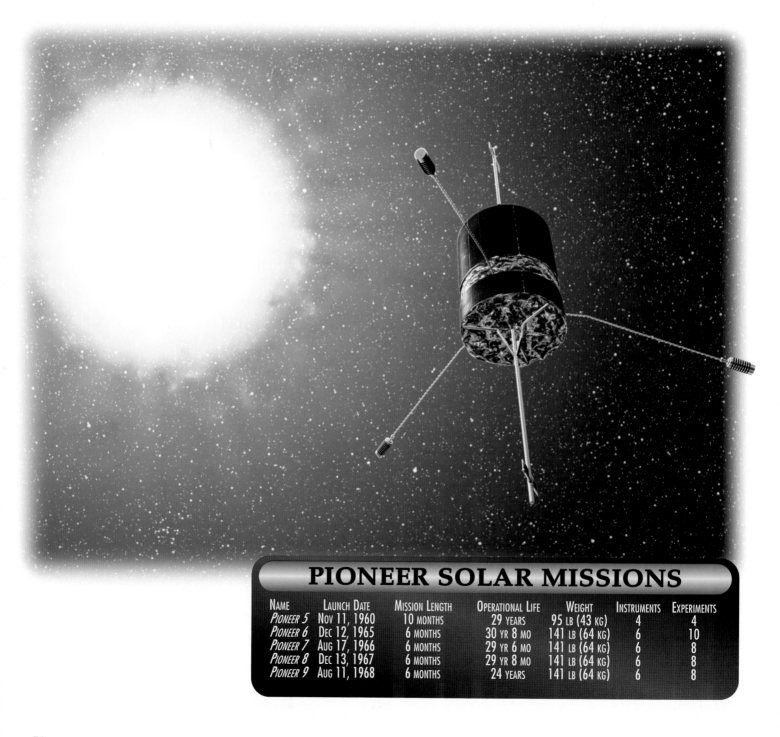

PIONEER SOLAR MISSIONS

Name	Launch Date	Mission Length	Operational Life	Weight	Instruments	Experiments
Pioneer 5	Nov 11, 1960	10 months	29 years	95 lb (43 kg)	4	4
Pioneer 6	Dec 12, 1965	6 months	30 yr 8 mo	141 lb (64 kg)	6	10
Pioneer 7	Aug 17, 1966	6 months	29 yr 6 mo	141 lb (64 kg)	6	8
Pioneer 8	Dec 13, 1967	6 months	29 yr 8 mo	141 lb (64 kg)	6	8
Pioneer 9	Aug 11, 1968	6 months	24 years	141 lb (64 kg)	6	8

SOLAR SUCCESS

The Pioneer program got off to a rocky start. Originally planned to be a series of lunar probes, only one of the first five Pioneer probes, *Pioneer 4*, made it anywhere near the Moon. Another of the early probes, *Pioneer 3*, discovered a second belt of trapped radiation around Earth—the first belt was discovered by the first US satellite, *Explorer 1*, in 1958. But these early Pioneers were largely regarded as failures. With the Moon proving difficult to reach, the next five Pioneer probes were designed to study the space between the Earth and the Sun, and they would do so with spectacular success.

On March 3, 1960, *Pioneer 5* was launched from Cape Canaveral. Once out in interplanetary space, the probe—which operated for 106 days—detected complex magnetic patterns. Like the earlier Pioneers, *Pioneer 5* carried an instrument to detect the levels of radiation trapped in the Earth's magnetic fields. The probe also carried two other high-energy particle detectors and a magnetic-field detector. It correlated changes in magnetic fields with the eruption of solar flares and proved that the Sun made space an extremely dangerous place for an unprotected astronaut.

The next Pioneer design, which lasted for four missions, was designed to investigate these intriguing electrical and magnetic phenomena in greater detail. After the early failures, the Pioneer program was finally ready to make some important contributions to the emerging field of space science.

EXTRA LONG LIFE

In addition to *Pioneer 5*'s instrumentation, *Pioneers 6* to *9* also had two instruments designed to measure the density of electrons in the solar wind. NASA's ingenious scientists even monitored changes in the probe's tracking signal to glean information about the wind the transmission passed through. All this information allowed for a better understanding of the structure and flow of the solar wind.

Among the new technology tested on the Pioneer probes was a gyroscope-type stabilization system. Like a spinning top or a

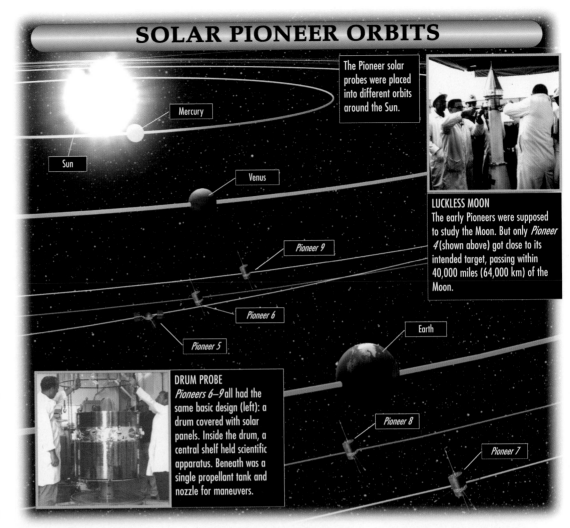

SOLAR PIONEER ORBITS

The Pioneer solar probes were placed into different orbits around the Sun.

Mercury

Sun

Venus

Pioneer 9

Pioneer 6

Pioneer 5

Earth

Pioneer 8

Pioneer 7

LUCKLESS MOON
The early Pioneers were supposed to study the Moon. But only *Pioneer 4* (shown above) got close to its intended target, passing within 40,000 miles (64,000 km) of the Moon.

DRUM PROBE
Pioneers 6–9 all had the same basic design (left): a drum covered with solar panels. Inside the drum, a central shelf held scientific apparatus. Beneath was a single propellant tank and nozzle for maneuvers.

rotating bicycle wheel, a space probe is less likely to wander off course if it is spinning. First used with the *Pioneer 6* probe, the technique proved so stable—the probe spun successfully at about 60 rpm—that it became standard on all NASA's subsequent deep-space probes.

Each of the next three Pioneers—*Pioneer 7* was launched in August 1966, *8* in December 1967, and *9* in November 1968—had a slightly different orbit so that a network of solar outposts

began to form. The probes allowed scientists to forecast solar storms accurately up to two weeks in advance—plenty of time to prepare to study the event. The solar network continued to operate until the early 1970s, providing a wealth of information about the complex electrical and magnetic lines that swirl around the Sun.

The satellites themselves operated far longer than the network. The youngest satellite, *Pioneer 9*, was the first to go—it

stopped transmitting in 1983. The other three probes held on for another decade. NASA's Deep Space Network last made contact with *Pioneer 7* in 1995, when only one of its instruments was still working. The story was the same for *Pioneer 8*, contacted a year later. Most surprising of all was the oldest sibling, *Pioneer 6*, which was still sending back data in 2000. Launched in 1977, *Voyager 2* has made it into the record books as NASA's oldest operational probe, still transmitting data in March 2014.

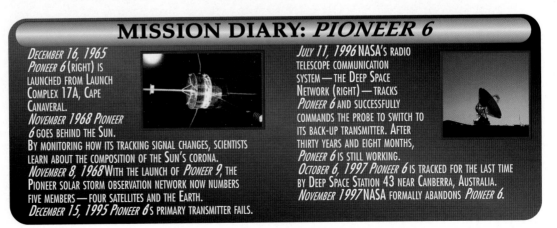

MISSION DIARY: *PIONEER 6*

DECEMBER 16, 1965 *PIONEER 6* (RIGHT) IS LAUNCHED FROM LAUNCH COMPLEX 17A, CAPE CANAVERAL.
NOVEMBER 1968 *PIONEER 6* GOES BEHIND THE SUN. BY MONITORING HOW ITS TRACKING SIGNAL CHANGES, SCIENTISTS LEARN ABOUT THE COMPOSITION OF THE SUN'S CORONA.
NOVEMBER 8, 1968 WITH THE LAUNCH OF *PIONEER 9*, THE PIONEER SOLAR STORM OBSERVATION NETWORK NOW NUMBERS FIVE MEMBERS — FOUR SATELLITES AND THE EARTH.
DECEMBER 15, 1995 *PIONEER 6*'S PRIMARY TRANSMITTER FAILS.

JULY 11, 1996 NASA'S RADIO TELESCOPE COMMUNICATION SYSTEM — THE DEEP SPACE NETWORK (RIGHT) — TRACKS *PIONEER 6* AND SUCCESSFULLY COMMANDS THE PROBE TO SWITCH TO ITS BACK-UP TRANSMITTER. AFTER THIRTY YEARS AND EIGHT MONTHS, *PIONEER 6* IS STILL WORKING.
OCTOBER 6, 1997 *PIONEER 6* IS TRACKED FOR THE LAST TIME BY DEEP SPACE STATION 43 NEAR CANBERRA, AUSTRALIA.
NOVEMBER 1997 NASA FORMALLY ABANDONS *PIONEER 6*.

PIONEER
10 AND *11*

Pioneer *10* and *11* are humanity's first emissaries to the galaxy at large. Launched in the early 1970s to investigate Jupiter and Saturn, they were the first spacecraft designed to leave the solar system behind. Now, they are more than seven billion miles (11,265,408,000 km) from home and still traveling outward through space. *Pioneer 11*'s power ran down in 1995, but *Pioneer 10*—officially retired—made contact with NASA in 2003 and may still be transmitting although communications are now down. Should either one encounter an alien race in the vastness of interstellar space, each carries a message from humanity.

PIONEER 10 AND *11*

MANUFACTURER	TRW	COMMUNICATIONS RATE	16–2,048 BPS THROUGH NASA DSN STATIONS
DESIGN LIFETIME	2.5 YEARS		
ANTENNA DIAMETER	8 FT 10 IN (2.6 M)	INSTRUMENTS CARRIED	
CURRENT SPEED, *PIONEER 10*	242M MILES/389M KM PER YEAR	MAGNETOMETER, PLASMA ANALYZER, CHARGED PARTICLE DETECTOR, IONIZING DETECTOR, NON-IMAGING TELESCOPES WITH OVERLAPPING FIELDS OF VIEW TO DETECT SUNLIGHT REFLECTED FROM PASSING METEOROIDS, MICROMETEOROID DETECTORS, UV PHOTOMETER, IR RADIOMETER, AND AN IMAGING PHOTOPOLARIMETER. *PIONEER 11* ALSO CARRIED A LOW-SENSITIVITY FLUXGATE MAGNETOMETER.	
CURRENT SPEED, *PIONEER 11*	232M MILES/372M KM PER YEAR		
ONBOARD POWER	RTGS (RADIOISOTOPE THERMONUCLEAR GENERATORS) PROVIDING 155 W		

DISTANT TRAVELERS

Pioneer 10 left for Jupiter on March 3, 1972. It was the latest in a long line of Pioneer probes designed to explore interplanetary space. At Jupiter's distance from the Sun, *Pioneer 10* and its sibling *Pioneer 11* could not rely on solar cells for energy. Instead, they carried a nuclear generator that drew power from the heat produced by radioactive plutonium. The most visible feature of both craft was an umbrella-like antenna 9 feet (2.75 m) across, needed to transmit data to Earth and to receive instructions from Mission Control. These instructions were vital—1970s computers were too heavy for the probes to carry, so there were no onboard brains. Instead, controllers had to put up with the fact that the probes would be so far distant that radio signals would take an hour and a half to reach them.

Pioneer 10, spinning five times a minute to stabilize its antenna, plunged into the asteroid belt beyond Mars in mid-July 1972, and emerged unharmed in February 1973. The project scientists had worried that it would be crippled or destroyed by a 30,000-miles-per-hour (50,000 kmh) collision with an interplanetary pebble, but *Pioneer 10*'s survival gave them the confidence to launch *Pioneer 11* in its wake.

Pioneer 10 began its encounter with Jupiter on November 26, 1973, when its instruments registered the presence of the giant planet's stormy magnetosphere. In the twenty-six days of its flypast, the little probe was battered by the intense radiation belts that surround Jupiter. As *Pioneer* skimmed past the planet, 81,000 miles (130,000 km) above the cloud tops, its instruments turned on Jupiter's most striking feature—the Great Red Spot. *Pioneer*'s pictures confirmed that the spot was in fact a giant storm. Its encounter over, *Pioneer 10* headed out of the solar system at 25,000 miles per hour (40,000 kmh) and passed the orbit of Pluto in 1990.

After *Pioneer 10*'s success, there seemed no need to repeat the same program. *Pioneer 11* was given a course correction that pointed it toward Jupiter's south pole rather than its equator, and took the spacecraft much closer to the planet than its predecessor— only 21,000 miles (33,796 kmh) above the clouds. As *Pioneer 11* whipped past, Jupiter's gravity accelerated the probe to a speed of 107,373 miles per hour (172,800 kmh) and flung it onward to a second planetary encounter— with Saturn. At Saturn, *Pioneer 11* swung past only 1,200 miles (1,931 km) from the ring system, and 13,000 miles (20,920 km) above the clouds. It discovered that Saturn had radiation belts and a strong magnetic field, found two new rings and a moon,

and helped scientists understand much more about the structure and composition of the gas giant. Its mission completed, *Pioneer 11* also headed out of the solar system, heading in the opposite direction to its predecessor.

SNAPSHOTS

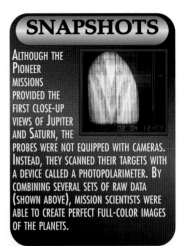

Although the Pioneer missions provided the first close-up views of Jupiter and Saturn, the probes were not equipped with cameras. Instead, they scanned their targets with a device called a photopolarimeter. By combining several sets of raw data (shown above), mission scientists were able to create perfect full-color images of the planets.

MISSION DIARY: *PIONEER 10* AND *11*

March 3, 1972 Pioneer 10 launched from Cape Canaveral on Atlas-Centaur booster.
July 1972–February 1973 Pioneer 10 successfully traverses the asteroid belt between Mars and Jupiter.
April 6, 1973 Pioneer 11 launched.
November 26, 1973 Pioneer 10 passes within Sinope's orbit, Jupiter's outermost known moon.
December 4, 1973, 6:26 p.m. Pioneer 10's closest approach to Jupiter, 81,000 miles (130,000 km) above the planet's clouds.
December 3, 1974 Pioneer 11's closest approach to Jupiter 26,725 miles (43,000 km).

September 1, 1979 Pioneer 11's closest approach to Saturn, at 13,000 miles (20,920 km).
June 13, 1983 Pioneer 10 crosses the orbit of Neptune (then the outermost planet due to the eccentricity of Pluto's orbit) and becomes the first craft to leave the solar system.
February 23, 1990 Pioneer 11 leaves the solar system.
September 22, 1990 Pioneer 10 reaches fifty times the Earth's distance from the Sun.

November 1995 Last communications received from Pioneer 11.
March 31, 1997 Formal end of Pioneer missions.
February 17, 1998 Voyager 1 spacecraft overtakes Pioneer 10 to become most distant human object.
2 million CE Pioneer 10 reaches the neighborhood of the red star Aldebaran.
4 million CE Pioneer 11 makes a close approach to a small star in the constellation Aquila (above).

ONWARD AND OUTWARD

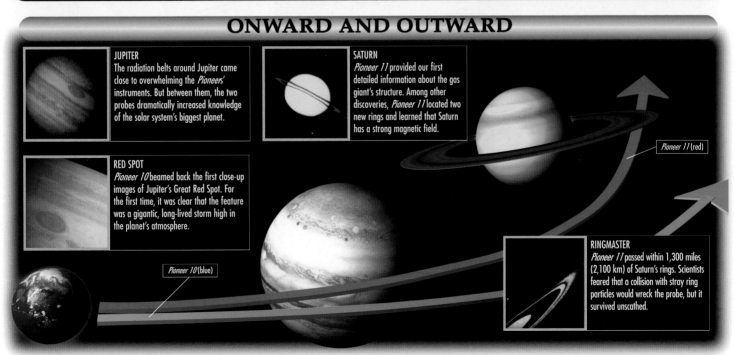

JUPITER
The radiation belts around Jupiter came close to overwhelming the *Pioneers'* instruments. But between them, the two probes dramatically increased knowledge of the solar system's biggest planet.

RED SPOT
Pioneer 10 beamed back the first close-up images of Jupiter's Great Red Spot. For the first time, it was clear that the feature was a gigantic, long-lived storm high in the planet's atmosphere.

Pioneer 10 (blue)

SATURN
Pioneer 11 provided our first detailed information about the gas giant's structure. Among other discoveries, *Pioneer 11* located two new rings and learned that Saturn has a strong magnetic field.

Pioneer 11 (red)

RINGMASTER
Pioneer 11 passed within 1,300 miles (2,100 km) of Saturn's rings. Scientists feared that a collision with stray ring particles would wreck the probe, but it survived unscathed.

VOYAGER MISSIONS

The twin spacecraft *Voyager 1* and *2* have transformed our understanding of the outer solar system. Originally designed to study only Jupiter and Saturn, these two intrepid probes have visited all the gas giants—Jupiter, Saturn, Uranus, and Neptune. They have sent back many startling images of churning atmospheres, complex ring systems, and exotic moons, some of which are large enough to be worlds in their own right. Now, as the Voyagers head for the stars, they continue to report from the very edge of the solar system, with *Voyager 1* the first man-made object to enter interstellar space.

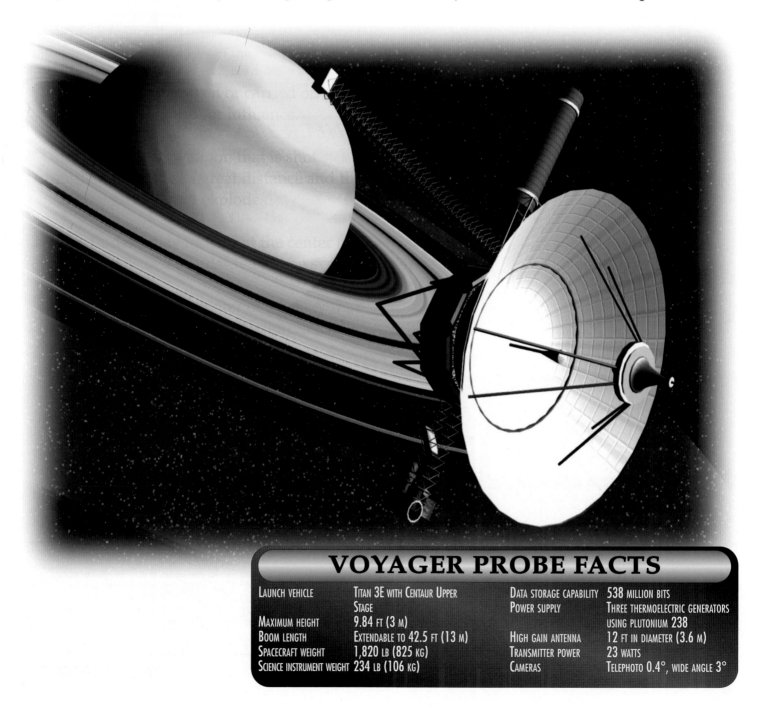

VOYAGER PROBE FACTS

LAUNCH VEHICLE	TITAN 3E WITH CENTAUR UPPER STAGE	DATA STORAGE CAPABILITY	538 MILLION BITS
		POWER SUPPLY	THREE THERMOELECTRIC GENERATORS USING PLUTONIUM 238
MAXIMUM HEIGHT	9.84 FT (3 M)		
BOOM LENGTH	EXTENDABLE TO 42.5 FT (13 M)	HIGH GAIN ANTENNA	12 FT IN DIAMETER (3.6 M)
SPACECRAFT WEIGHT	1,820 LB (825 KG)	TRANSMITTER POWER	23 WATTS
SCIENCE INSTRUMENT WEIGHT	234 LB (106 KG)	CAMERAS	TELEPHOTO 0.4°, WIDE ANGLE 3°

THE GRAND TOUR

Voyager 1 and *2* set off on their epic journeys of discovery in 1977. Their launches were timed to take advantage of a rare planetary alignment. Every 176 years, the giant planets of the outer solar system are aligned in such a way that a well-aimed spacecraft can use their gravitational fields to slingshot its way from one to the other. After each encounter, the spacecraft picks up speed—enough to have reached Neptune by 1989 in the case of *Voyager 2*. Without such boosts, the trip would have taken at least thirty years.

First port of call on the "Grand Tour" was Jupiter. *Voyager 1* got there first, in the spring of 1979, followed by its sister ship in July of the same year. The two probes investigated Jupiter's Great Red Spot, found a previously undiscovered ring system, and even detected powerful lightning bolts on the planet.

Hurled onward to Saturn by Jupiter's gravity, the Voyagers reached the planet in 1981 and beamed back our first detailed pictures of its intricate system of rings and moons. *Voyager 1* made a close flyby of the moon Titan, where it found an atmosphere denser than the Earth's. But the Titan mission was the spacecraft's last: the moon's gravity swung *Voyager 1* high above the ecliptic (the orbital plane of the solar system) and onward into interstellar space.

Voyager 2 continued to Uranus and sent back images of a planet that up until then had been little more than a blank disk to earthbound astronomers. At Neptune, the spacecraft passed within 3,000 miles (4,800 km) of the surface, its closest approach to any planet since it had left Earth. Its last encounter was with Neptune's largest moon, Triton. There, almost 3 billion miles (4.8 billion km) from the Sun, *Voyager 2* made the totally unexpected discovery of ice volcanoes. The probes were still in contact up to September 2013, when *Voyager 1* entered interstellar space.

MISSION DIARY: VOYAGER

AUGUST 20, 1977 *VOYAGER 2* IS LAUNCHED FROM CAPE CANAVERAL. SEPTEMBER 5, 1977 *VOYAGER 1* IS LAUNCHED FROM THE CAPE SIXTEEN DAYS LATER (ABOVE RIGHT). MARCH 5, 1979 *VOYAGER 1* REACHES JUPITER. EN ROUTE, IT OVERTOOK *VOYAGER 2* AND JUSTIFIED ITS DESIGNATION. JULY 9, 1979 *VOYAGER 2* MAKES A FLYBY OF JUPITER ON A COMPLEMENTARY COURSE TO *VOYAGER 1*. IT MAKES A CLOSE APPROACH TO THE MOON EUROPA AND INVESTIGATES JUPITER'S SOUTHERN LATITUDES. NOVEMBER 12, 1980 *VOYAGER 1* PASSES SATURN. AFTER A CLOSE ENCOUNTER WITH TITAN, IT IS HURLED OFF-COURSE BY TITAN'S GRAVITY. AUGUST 26, 1981 *VOYAGER 2* PLUNGES

THROUGH SATURN'S RINGS (RIGHT) AND PICKS UP ENOUGH SPEED FROM ITS GRAVITY TO CARRY ON TO URANUS. JANUARY 24, 1986 *VOYAGER 2* SURVEYS URANUS AND ITS MANY SATELLITES. AUGUST 25, 1989 *VOYAGER 2* PHOTOGRAPHS THE COLDEST PLACE TO BE FOUND SO FAR FOUND IN THE SOLAR SYSTEM — THE SURFACE OF NEPTUNE'S LARGEST MOON TRITON (BELOW).

TRAVEL SNAPSHOTS

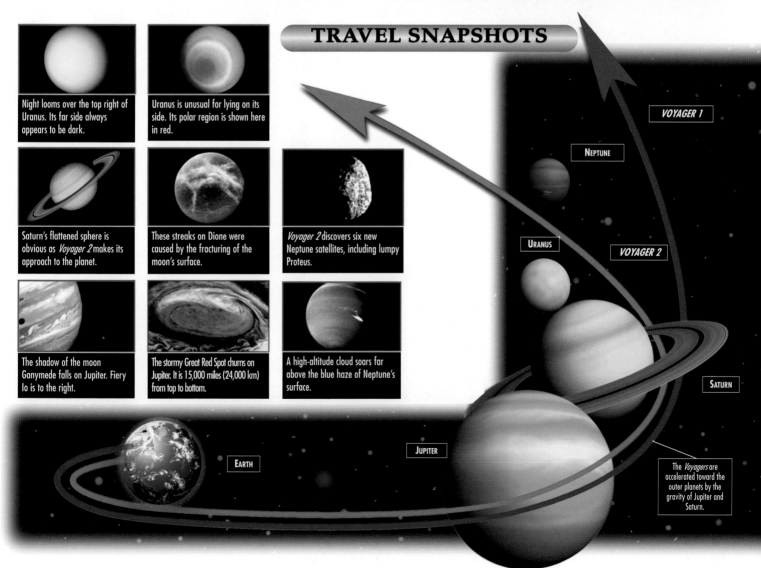

Night looms over the top right of Uranus. Its far side always appears to be dark.

Uranus is unusual for lying on its side. Its polar region is shown here in red.

Saturn's flattened sphere is obvious as *Voyager 2* makes its approach to the planet.

These streaks on Dione were caused by the fracturing of the moon's surface.

Voyager 2 discovers six new Neptune satellites, including lumpy Proteus.

The shadow of the moon Ganymede falls on Jupiter. Fiery Io is to the right.

The stormy Great Red Spot churns on Jupiter. It is 15,000 miles (24,000 km) from top to bottom.

A high-altitude cloud soars far above the blue haze of Neptune's surface.

VOYAGER 1

NEPTUNE

URANUS

VOYAGER 2

SATURN

EARTH

JUPITER

The *Voyagers* are accelerated toward the outer planets by the gravity of Jupiter and Saturn.

DEEP SPACE 1

Deep Space 1 is a revolutionary new spacecraft. It is powered by a new, super-efficient engine and carries an intelligent computer that pilots the craft with minimal instructions from ground control. The mission of this little probe is to test out these and other new—and potentially high-risk—technologies in space. It is the first spaceflight NASA has launched purely to test innovations. It is part of NASA's New Millennium Program, which will help shape the spacecraft of the future.

DS1 SPECIFICATIONS

Total Cost	$152.3M (FY95-99)	High Gain Antenna Diameter	11 in (28 cm)
Launch Date	October 24, 1998	Communications Frequencies	X, Ka
Launch Site	Cape Canaveral, Florida	Maximum Data Rate	20 kilobits per second
End of Mission Date	December 2001	Maximum Power	2,500W (2,100W used to power ion engine)
Launch Mass (spacecraft and propellants)	1072.13 lb (486.3 kg)		

SPACE GUINEA PIG

When it blasted into orbit aboard a Delta rocket on October 28, 1998, *Deep Space 1* (*DS1*) carried on board no fewer than twelve new technologies for testing. Some will make the spacecraft of the future smaller and cheaper; others aim to increase the precision of space astronomy. But the key innovations aboard *DS1* are its engine and its control system.

DS1 is propelled by an ion engine. In a chemical rocket like the Space Shuttle, a continuous controlled explosion hurls burning gas out of the rocket nozzle, driving the vehicle onward and upward. An ion engine is somewhat more sedate. Instead of a chemical reaction, it uses electric power to accelerate charged particles of gas out of the engine nozzle. Instead of thundering sheets of flame, the ion engine produces an eerie blue glow. And instead of hundreds of tons of thrust, the ion engine produces a thrust of just one third of an ounce (0.275 N)—or about one-tenth of the weight of an apple.

But appearances can be misleading. Ion engines are deceptively powerful and extremely efficient. They can go on producing thrust continuously for months on end. *Deep Space 1*'s supply of 180 pounds (82 kg) of xenon gas is enough to provide thrust continuously for twenty months, during which time the engine will have gradually accelerated the spacecraft up to speeds of 10,000 miles per hour (16,000 kmh).

SOLAR-POWERED IONS

The ion engine is powered by an array of solar cells. At full throttle, the engine consumes 2.5 kilowatts of power—about the same as a large electric heater. This is a great deal of power to generate using solar cells, so *Deep Space 1* is testing a new type of high-powered solar array. The spacecraft has two "wings," each one measuring 14 feet 9 inches (4.5 m) by 5 feet 3 inches (1.6 m) in size and composed of 360 silicon lenses that focus sunlight onto 1,800 solar cells. These "solar concentrator arrays" yield up to 20 percent more power than the best existing solar cell designs.

Deep Space 1's sophisticated automatic pilot system is just as ground-breaking as its revolutionary engine. It makes *DS1* virtually independent of NASA's tracking network and ground controllers. The system has two main components. The first, AutoNav, can determine exactly where *DS1* is in the solar system so that the probe can fine-tune its own flight path. To do this, it carries a database of the orbits of 250 asteroids and the positions of 250,000 background stars. By regularly taking pictures of asteroids and comparing the images to its stored data, *DS1* can calculate its own position and adjust the thrust of its ion engine as required. The second component of the control system is a piece of software called "Remote Agent." NASA ground controllers feed only very general instructions into Remote Agent. The software then calculates not only how it should carry out the orders, but also the best sequence in which to execute them.

While there were some issues with the major new technologies aboard *DS1*, most outperformed expectations. The craft's failures have been educational and its successes have set the stage for future ion-propelled missions.

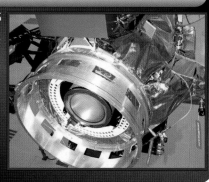

CLEAN FUEL

THE ION DRIVE POWERING *DS1* IS THE MOST EFFICIENT ENGINE EVER FLOWN IN SPACE — HUNDREDS OF TIMES MORE SO THAN THE SPACE SHUTTLE ENGINES, WHICH REQUIRED HUGE RESERVES OF FUEL. BUT WHERE EACH OF THOSE MONSTERS PRODUCES AROUND 200 TONS (181 T) OF THRUST, THE THRUST FROM *DS1*'S ION ENGINE IS LITTLE MORE THAN THE WEIGHT OF A SINGLE SHEET OF PAPER.

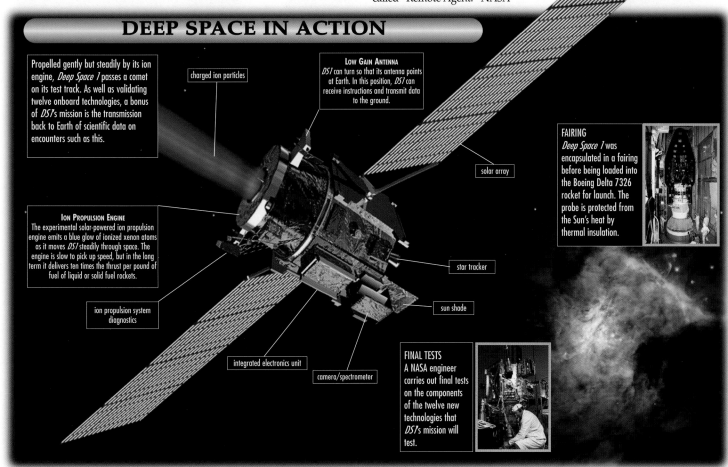

DEEP SPACE IN ACTION

Propelled gently but steadily by its ion engine, *Deep Space 1* passes a comet on its test track. As well as validating twelve onboard technologies, a bonus of *DS1*'s mission is the transmission back to Earth of scientific data on encounters such as this.

charged ion particles

LOW GAIN ANTENNA
DS1 can turn so that its antenna points at Earth. In this position, *DS1* can receive instructions and transmit data to the ground.

solar array

FAIRING
Deep Space 1 was encapsulated in a fairing before being loaded into the Boeing Delta 7326 rocket for launch. The probe is protected from the Sun's heat by thermal insulation.

ION PROPULSION ENGINE
The experimental solar-powered ion propulsion engine emits a blue glow of ionized xenon atoms as it moves *DS1* steadily through space. The engine is slow to pick up speed, but in the long term it delivers ten times the thrust per pound of fuel of liquid or solid fuel rockets.

ion propulsion system diagnostics

star tracker

sun shade

integrated electronics unit

camera/spectrometer

FINAL TESTS
A NASA engineer carries out final tests on the components of the twelve new technologies that *DS1*'s mission will test.

CASSINI-HUYGENS

A quarter of a century after *Pioneer 11* took the first close-up pictures of Saturn, the ringed planet came under the gaze of a new NASA craft. The massive *Cassini-Huygens* spacecraft reached Jupiter in 2000. In December 2004, the *Huygens* probe—released from *Cassini*—plunged into the thick atmosphere of Saturn's moon Titan, sending back enough data to keep scientists busy for decades. The $3.25 billion project is set to be the last big-budget probe mission for some time. And if all goes according to plan, it should also be one of the longest in duration, with extensions currently planned until 2017.

CASSINI-HUYGENS STATS

	Cassini Orbiter	*Huygens* Probe
Number of instruments	18	7
Power generation	PLUTONIUM THERMOELECTRIC GENERATORS	LITHIUM SULFUR DIOXIDE BATTERIES
Unfueled navigation	GRAVITY ASSISTS	GRAVITY, PARACHUTES
Fueled navigation	TWO 100-LB-FORCE (440 N) THRUSTERS	THREE 112-LB-FORCE (498 N) SPRINGS
Propellant	MONO-METHYL-HYDRAZINE, NITROGEN TETROXIDE	NONE
Unfueled weight	4,750 LB (2,154 KG)	770 LB (349 KG)
Weight of fuel	6,905 LB (3,132 KG)	NONE
Dimensions	22 FT (6.7 M) HIGH, 13 FT (4 M) WIDE	9 FT (2.7 M) IN DIAMETER
Duration of mission	43 MONTHS	3 HOURS

SATURN SAILOR

After its long journey from Earth, *Cassini* made its closest approach to Jupiter on December 30, 2000, and began taking measurements and photographs. In all, 26,000 images of Jupiter were taken, allowing for the creation of the most detailed global portrait ever made of the planet.

One area of new study was the rings of Jupiter, barely visible from Earth. *Cassini* showed that they were made of irregular, rather than spherical particles, suggesting they were ejected from Jupiter's moons Metis and Adrastea by micrometeorite impacts.

The scientific discoveries of *Cassini* are almost too numerous to describe. Among them are two new moons of Saturn, spotted in June 2004. These bodies are very small, but have been named Methone and Pallene (after two sisters from Greek mythology).

Direct observation of the planets and moons of the outer solar system was only one area of study. The *Cassini* science team took the opportunity to put Einstein's theory of general relativity to the test. They experimented with radio signals from *Cassini* to prove that a massive object like the Sun causes space-time to curve, and a beam of radio waves or light that passes by the Sun has to travel farther because of the curvature and the delay in reaching Earth can be used to measure the amount of curve. Results from *Cassini* have not conclusively proved the theory, but have increased scientific confidence in it greatly.

The most spectacular experiment conducted by *Cassini* was the despatch of the *Huygens* probe to the surface of Titan. After a large number of preliminary flybys, *Cassini* ejected *Huygens* towards Titan on December 25, 2004, although it didn't arrive for a further three weeks.

As *Huygens* entered Titan's atmosphere it sent data and images to Earth via *Cassini*. Betting that the landing site was as likely to be liquid methane as solid rock, the probe was designed to float. With a battery life of only three hours, most of which would be taken up with the descent, only thirty minutes of surface data was expected.

As it fell toward Titan suspended on a parachute, photos were transmitted of what looked like a shoreline and islands. Methane clouds or haze were also seen before the probe plopped into a clay-like material described as "Titanian Mud." The color of Titan's surface was described as orange or "creme brulee."

An operator mistake in forgetting to turn on *Cassini*'s receiver for one of two *Huygens* data channels led to the loss of all measurements of descent winds, and of three hundred fifty of the seven hundred images taken before landing. Nonetheless, the probe survived on the surface where it transmitted data for over an hour and twelve minutes. It is regarded as a great success.

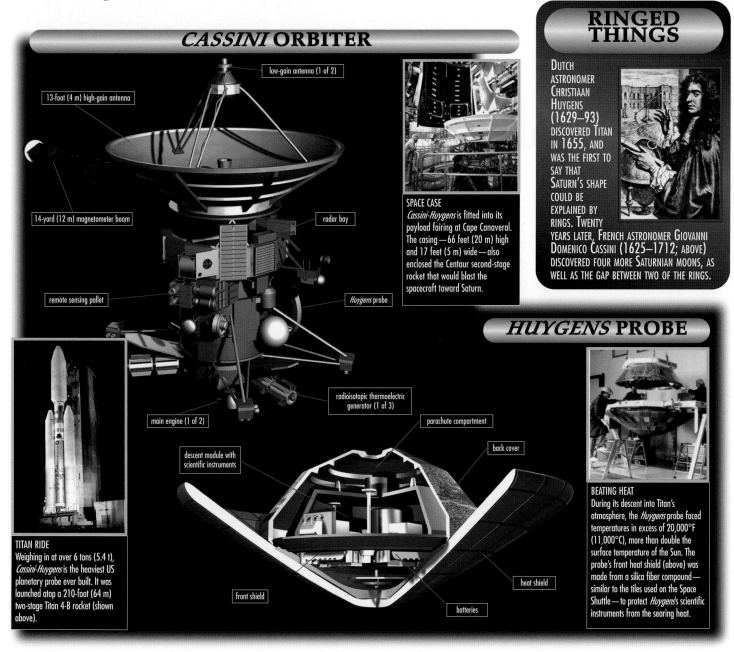

CASSINI ORBITER

low-gain antenna (1 of 2)

13-foot (4 m) high-gain antenna

14-yard (12 m) magnetometer boom

radar bay

remote sensing pallet

Huygens probe

main engine (1 of 2)

radioisotopic thermoelectric generator (1 of 3)

parachute compartment

back cover

descent module with scientific instruments

front shield

batteries

heat shield

SPACE CASE
Cassini-Huygens is fitted into its payload fairing at Cape Canaveral. The casing—66 feet (20 m) high and 17 feet (5 m) wide—also enclosed the Centaur second-stage rocket that would blast the spacecraft toward Saturn.

RINGED THINGS

Dutch astronomer Christiaan Huygens (1629–93) discovered Titan in 1655, and was the first to say that Saturn's shape could be explained by rings. Twenty years later, French astronomer Giovanni Domenico Cassini (1625–1712; above) discovered four more Saturnian moons, as well as the gap between two of the rings.

HUYGENS PROBE

TITAN RIDE
Weighing in at over 6 tons (5.4 t), *Cassini-Huygens* is the heaviest US planetary probe ever built. It was launched atop a 210-foot (64 m) two-stage Titan 4-B rocket (shown above).

BEATING HEAT
During its descent into Titan's atmosphere, the *Huygens* probe faced temperatures in excess of 20,000°F (11,000°C), more than double the surface temperature of the Sun. The probe's front heat shield (above) was made from a silica fiber compound—similar to the tiles used on the Space Shuttle—to protect *Huygens*'s scientific instruments from the searing heat.

LOST PROBES

Exploration has always had its dangers, and exploring space presents many hazards to the robotic spacecraft that have been sent out to investigate the mysteries of the solar system. These probes have to survive the extremely hostile environment of space, often for long periods of time, and despite their usually reliable technology, they occasionally break down and are never heard from again. But each failure teaches spacecraft designers valuable lessons that will help to improve the success rate of future missions.

SPACECRAFT LOSSES

MOON MISSIONS					
LUNA 1	USSR	SURVEYOR 4	US	PHOBOS 1	RUSSIA
PIONEER 4	US	LUNA 18	USSR	PHOBOS 2	RUSSIA
RANGER 3	US			MARS OBSERVER	US
RANGER 4	US	MARS MISSIONS		CLIMATE ORBITER	US
RANGER 5	US	MARS 1	USSR	POLAR LANDER	US
LUNA 4	USSR	ZOND 2	USSR	BEAGLE 2	UK
RANGER 6	US	MARS 2	USSR	YINGHUO-1	CHINA
LUNA 6	USSR	MARS 3	USSR	FOBOS-GRUNT	RUSSIA
		MARS 6	USSR		

VENUS MISSIONS	
VENERA 1	USSR
ZOND 1	USSR
VENERA 2	USSR
VENERA 3	USSR

LOST IN SPACE

Since the very earliest days of spaceflight, probes have been launched out into the solar system. The Moon was the first target, since the US and the Soviet Union needed to gather data and accumulate technical experience in preparation for crewed lunar missions. And with the Cold War rivalry between the two superpowers increasing, each tried to prove they had the world's best technology. Missions to Mars and Venus soon followed the first Moonshots.

But in the early 1960s, so little was known of conditions in space that many satellites and probes failed within days of launch. To reach Mars or Venus, a spacecraft had to survive a flight lasting nine months or more, so the probes had to be highly reliable. This was achieved by adding backup systems that would take over if a primary system failed. Backups could be supplied for most of the essential functions of the spacecraft, but there were always a small number of components and systems whose failure would end the mission. Such devices had "single-point criticality."

The largest single-point-critical element in any space mission is the launcher. If the booster fails during ascent to orbit, the mission ends before it has even left the Earth. And even when it has safely entered its interplanetary trajectory, a spacecraft still faces dangers meaning it might malfunction. For instance, a computer or thruster failure can leave the spacecraft facing in the wrong direction, so that its communication antenna loses contact with the Earth.

LEARNING FROM FAILURES

Although many missions have been lost, their scientific instruments have usually managed to return a small amount of information before failure. Using this data, scientists have been able to understand the space environment more, which in turn has helped engineers to improve probe design. As designs have improved, so has the success rate, but failures have by no means been eliminated.

In preparation for the human exploration of Mars, NASA has once again turned its attention to that planet. Two spacecraft are sent during each launch window but problems have plagued almost every flight. During the 1990s, Mars *Pathfinder* was a success but Mars *Observer*, Mars *Climate Orbiter*, and Mars *Polar Lander* were all lost. Mars *Polar Lander* disappeared in December 1999. It probably reached the surface of the planet, but no signals were ever received from it. But new interplanetary missions are currently underway.

DATA BLOCK

Soon after the 1989 launch of *Galileo* (right) to Jupiter, controllers feared they would lose the spacecraft when its main antenna failed to deploy properly. A later problem with a tape recorder also jeopardized the mission. By uploading new software, NASA retrieved most of the craft's scientific data, but its data transmission rate was less than a ten thousandth of its planned 134 kilobits per second.

PROBES TO MARS AND VENUS

MARS 1
The first mission to fly past Mars was the Soviet *Mars 1* probe, launched in 1962. It probably got to within 118,000 miles (191,000 km) of Mars in June 1963, but all contact with it had been lost in March.

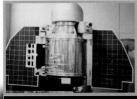

PHOBOS PROBES
In 1985, the Soviet Union sent a pair of probes to study Phobos, one of the moons of Mars. But contact with *Phobos 1* was lost before it reached Mars, and *Phobos 2* was lost shortly after it entered Mars orbit.

Most of the interplanetary probes that have been launched—and most of those that have been lost—were headed for our nearest planetary neighbors, Mars and Venus.

MARS

VENERAS
The Soviet Venera missions to Venus got off to a bad start in the 1960s with the loss of the first probe in 1961 and the second and third in 1964. But *Veneras 4* (in 1967) through *16* (in 1981) were successful.

THE MOON

EARTH

SURVEYOR '98
The ill-fated and costly Mars *Surveyor* of 1998 mission consisted of the Mars *Climate Orbiter* (top) and the Mars *Polar Lander* (bottom). The *Climate Orbiter* burned up in the Martian atmosphere in September 1999, and all contact with the *Polar Lander* was lost in December 1999.

VENUS

THE LOST ZONDS
The first two of the Soviet Zond series of probes were lost due to communications failure. These were *Zond 1*, on a mission to Venus that launched on April 2, 1964, and the *Zond 2* Mars probe, which launched on November 30, 1964.

NEW HORIZONS

On the first ever NASA mission to reach Pluto and beyond, *New Horizons* made history when the probe reached dwarf planet's system on July 14, 2015. This historic mission was ten years in the making before the successful launch on January 19, 2006, meaning that it took almost another ten years for *New Horizons* to fulfill its mission objective and reach Pluto. The journey was measured at over 3 billion miles (4.8 billion km), but the probe has not not stopped there. Flying onward, it will explore objects within the Kuiper Belt on the very outskirts of our solar system.

NEW HORIZONS TRAJECTORY

Planets *New Horizons* has passed	Date
Mars	April 7, 2006
Jupiter	February 28, 2007
Saturn	June 8, 2008
Uranus	March 18, 2011
Neptune	August 25, 2014
Pluto	July 14, 2015

PROBING PLUTO AND BEYOND

By studying Pluto and the Kuiper Belt, the NASA space probe *New Horizons* will live up to its name. The probe's launch was delayed twice because of weather and power shortages in the days leading up to its successful launch. Cloud cover around the Cape Canaveral launch site on January 19 almost saw the highly anticipated launch delayed once more. Finally launched without further hitches in January 2006, *New Horizons* is the first probe to fly by, photograph, and study Pluto and its moons. The probe entered the Pluto-Charon system in July 2015, where it is studying the last unexplored planet in our solar system (Pluto was still classed as a planet when the study was proposed in early 2006). *New Horizons* flew within 6,000 miles (9,600 km) of Pluto in 2015. The probe is equipped with technology that will study the geology, surface composition, and atmosphere of Pluto in detail, as well as map as much of the dwarf planet and its major moon, Charon. At its closest, *New Horizons* photographed the ultraviolet emissions from Pluto's atmosphere to map the dwarf planet and Charon. Both bodies were photographed in detail, allowing images of objects around 200 feet (60 m) to be seen clearly for the first time.

New Horizons will go farther still into the Kuiper Belt. Here, the aim is to seek Kuiper Belt objects (KBO) of over 30 miles (50 km) to fly by, photograph, and observe. These KBOs need to be within a certain distance from Pluto for the probe to be able to successfully communicate its findings back to Earth. By December 2011, *New Horizons* had passed closer to Pluto than any other spacecraft, including *Voyager 1*, the probe that had previously held this record. While it is expected that the *New Horizons* mission will end in 2026, if the probe lasts until 2038, it will begin to probe the outer heliosphere of the solar system. It is thought unlikely that *New Horizons* will ever overtake the Voyager probes as the most distant man-made object from Earth.

New Horizons marks the first mission of New Frontiers, a NASA initiative that aims to reach Jupiter and Venus as well as Pluto. *New Horizons* was the first New Frontiers mission, with *Juno* launching in August 2011, aiming to reach Jupiter by 2016. The third mission, OSIRIS-REx, will study and return samples of an asteroid. It is due to launch in 2016.

SPIN CYCLE

After careful assembly of the craft, it is rigorously tested before launch. *New Horizons* and similar spacecrafts have to endure extreme conditions of heat and cold, as well as being flung at high speeds into various trajectories to remain on course. *New Horizons* is shaped like a triangle, with much of its equipment in a compartment within the outer structure. The radio dish and antenna are external so they can pick up signals with no interference. The titanium body was made big enough so that the equipment can travel safely and be shielded from radiation or electrical charges. As well as withstanding temperature extremes when traveling from the inner to outer solar system, *New Horizons* is a spinning spacecraft that is constantly in motion. Scientists needed to ensure that the sensitive equipment inside the probe remains safe so that data can be returned to Earth.

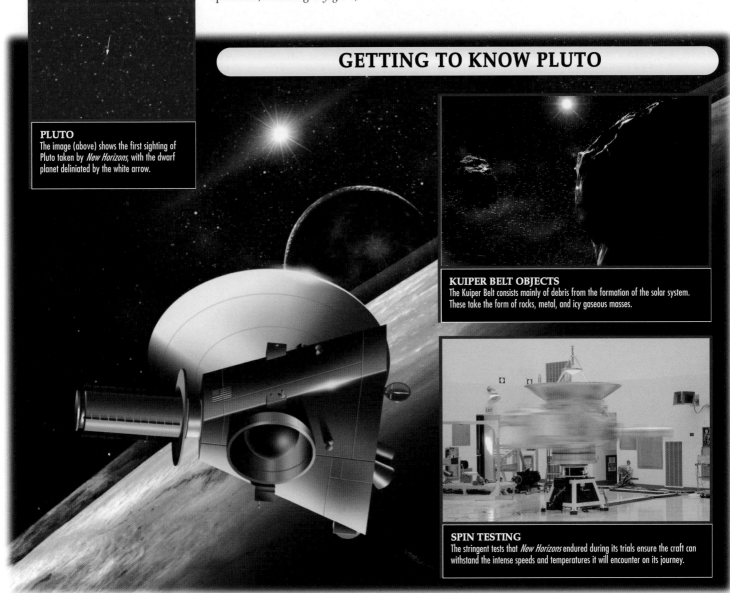

GETTING TO KNOW PLUTO

PLUTO
The image (above) shows the first sighting of Pluto taken by *New Horizons*, with the dwarf planet deliniated by the white arrow.

KUIPER BELT OBJECTS
The Kuiper Belt consists mainly of debris from the formation of the solar system. These take the form of rocks, metal, and icy gaseous masses.

SPIN TESTING
The stringent tests that *New Horizons* endured during its trials ensure the craft can withstand the intense speeds and temperatures it will encounter on its journey.

HERSCHEL SPACE OBSERVATORY

A space observatory built by the European Space Agency in 2009, Herschel consisted of the largest infrared telescope ever launched into space. Herschel was part of the ESA cornerstone science mission Horizon 2000, along with the Rosetta spacecraft, which was launched in 2004 to study the comet 67P and has just recently been awoken from sleep mode, and the Gaia observatory, launched on December 19, 2013 with the aim of creating a three-dimensional map of the Milky Way. Also launched, at the same time as Herschel in May 2009, was the Planck observatory. Herschel's mission was always somewhat limited by time, as the telescope relied on supplies of coolant. Despite its limited life span, Herschel was responsible for making thousands of enlightening observations as well as several exciting new discoveries.

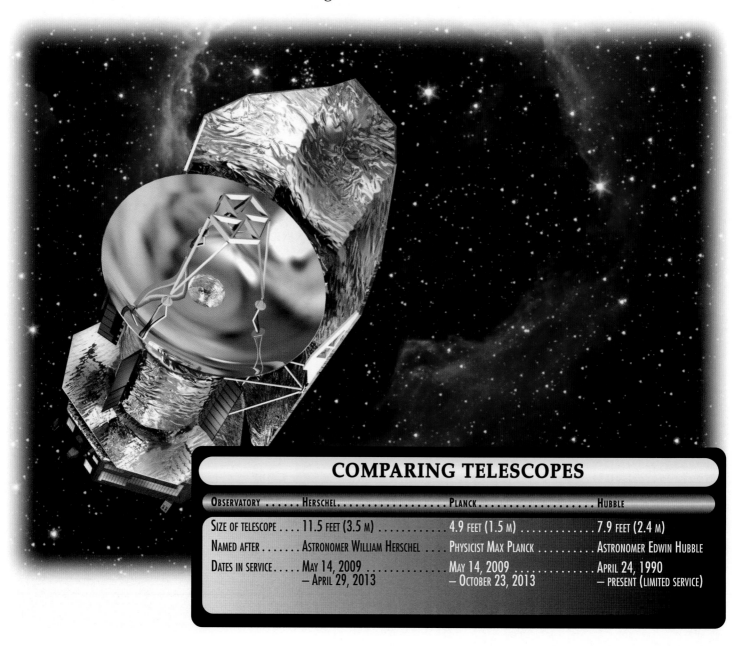

COMPARING TELESCOPES

Observatory	Herschel	Planck	Hubble
Size of telescope	11.5 feet (3.5 m)	4.9 feet (1.5 m)	7.9 feet (2.4 m)
Named after	Astronomer William Herschel	Physicist Max Planck	Astronomer Edwin Hubble
Dates in service	May 14, 2009 – April 29, 2013	May 14, 2009 – October 23, 2013	April 24, 1990 – present (limited service)

HERSCHEL TAKES TO THE SKIES

Operational from 2009 to 2013, the Herschel Space Observatory was operated by the ESA until April 29, 2013. Its estimated 3.5 year life was extended since its launch on May 15, 2009, but its coolant supply ran out after almost four years, rendering the Herschel observatory obsolete. Vital for the successful running of its instruments, this liquid helium coolant made it possible for the observatory to observe the formation of galaxies and stars throughout the solar system and Milky Way, as well as objects over billions of light-years away. The observatory has the capability to view wavelengths that have never been studied before.

Herschel was also the first observatory able to cover the full spectrum of infrared and sub-millimeter waves. Active since July 21, 2009, Herschel made over 37,000 scientific observations, including the discovery of an unknown stage in the process of star formation and confirmation of the presence of molecular oxygen in space.

Because of its infrared technology, Herschel is able to observe and photograph the "coolest and dustiest" objects in space. It was situated in solar orbit, in the second Langrangian point of the Earth-Sun system at a distance of 930,000 miles (1,500,000 km) from Earth—known as L2. This positioning means that Herschel will not suffer from distortions in temperature from repeatedly passing in and out of Earth's shadow, which also disturbs the view. At its vantage point, Herschel can observe cool areas that may become stars.

The observatory's mission aims included study of the formation and evolution of galaxies, interstellar medium, and the process of star formation, and study of the composition of the atmosphere and surfaces of celestial bodies, including planets, comets, and asteroids. In addition to its key aims and observations, Herschel will be available for experiments sent by scientists all over the world. Herschel includes the largest mirror ever used in a space telescope, which is made from the durable sintered silicone carbide instead of glass. The telescope was able to work at temperatures down to -456°F (-271°C). The coolant that eventually ran out was liquid helium. The store of over 528 gallons (2,000 liters) was the maximum the craft could hold and meant that Herschel could run for at least three years. In the end, it was closer to four years, and Herschel was deactivated before being launched safely into solar orbit.

NEW DISCOVERIES

Herschel began operating on July 21, 2009. Since its operational launch, Herschel has discovered a previously unknown galaxy, which has now been designated HFLS3. This starburst galaxy is thought to have come into existence around 880 million years after the Big Bang occured and is much bigger than most other galaxies of its age. It has been able to observe and shed light on a previously undiscovered step in the process of the formation of a star, and how star forming regions discard some of the matter that they are surrounded with. Herschel also detected cosmic microwave background (CMB) radiation caused by light bending as it travels across the universe and meets huge objects. This means scientists are one step closer to finding the earliest gravitational waves produced a millisecond after the universe came into being.

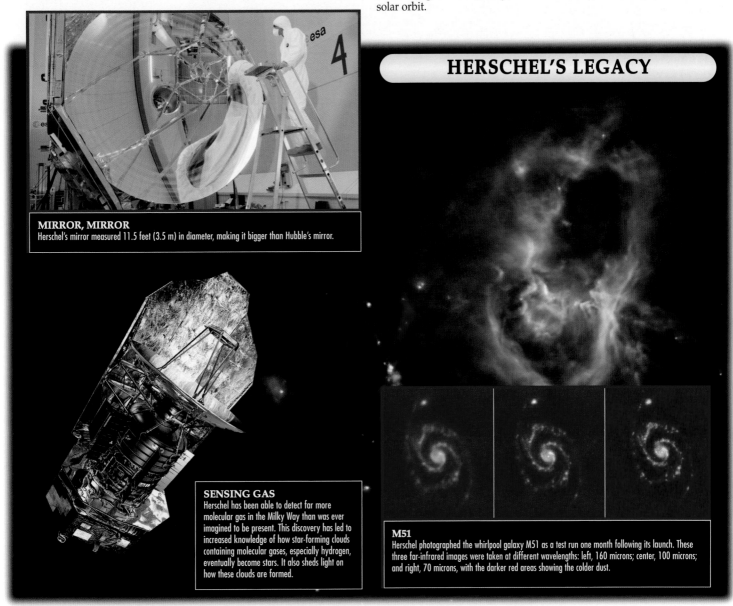

HERSCHEL'S LEGACY

MIRROR, MIRROR
Herschel's mirror measured 11.5 feet (3.5 m) in diameter, making it bigger than Hubble's mirror.

SENSING GAS
Herschel has been able to detect far more molecular gas in the Milky Way than was ever imagined to be present. This discovery has led to increased knowledge of how star-forming clouds containing molecular gases, especially hydrogen, eventually become stars. It also sheds light on how these clouds are formed.

M51
Herschel photographed the whirlpool galaxy M51 as a test run one month following its launch. These three far-infrared images were taken at different wavelengths: left, 160 microns; center, 100 microns; and right, 70 microns, with the darker red areas showing the colder dust.

PLANCK

The Planck observatory was launched to observe remaining radiation caused by the Big Bang, known as cosmic microwave background (CMB) radiation. While there have been similar operations, Planck was the first able to measure the temperature variations of this relic radiation with such sharp accuracy, meaning that theories on the evolution of the universe could be proven or disproved and that questions on the conditions for evolution could begin to be answered. It might even be impossible ever to better the images and data observed by Planck, as its level of accuracy is at the limit of astrophysics as we know it.

CMB OBSERVATORIES

Observatory	Location	Mission length	Mass
Planck	L2	4 years, 5 months	4,300 lb (1,950 kg)
WMAP	L2	12 years, 6 months	1,851 lb (840 kg)
COBE	Earth orbit	3 years, 11 months	5,005 lb (2,270 kg)

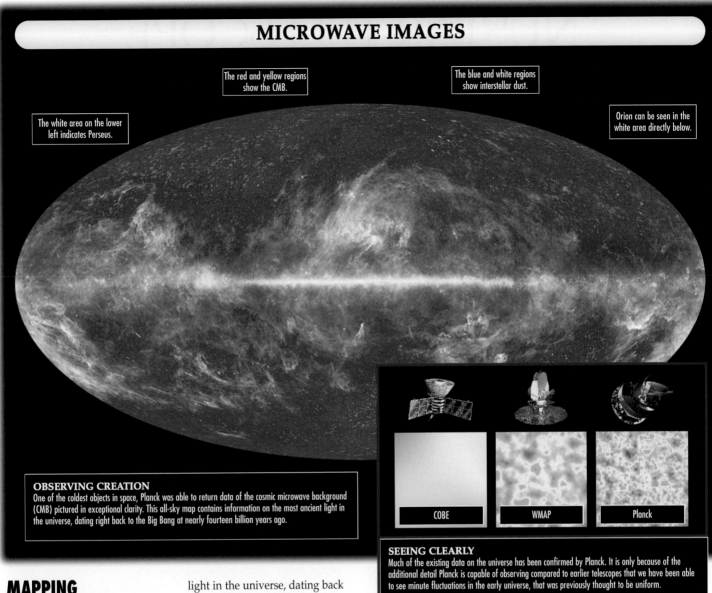

The red and yellow regions show the CMB.

The blue and white regions show interstellar dust.

The white area on the lower left indicates Perseus.

Orion can be seen in the white area directly below.

OBSERVING CREATION
One of the coldest objects in space, Planck was able to return data of the cosmic microwave background (CMB) pictured in exceptional clarity. This all-sky map contains information on the most ancient light in the universe, dating right back to the Big Bang at nearly fourteen billion years ago.

COBE

WMAP

Planck

SEEING CLEARLY
Much of the existing data on the universe has been confirmed by Planck. It is only because of the additional detail Planck is capable of observing compared to earlier telescopes that we have been able to see minute fluctuations in the early universe, that was previously thought to be uniform.

MAPPING MICROWAVES

Launched in 2009 by the ESA, Planck was initially called COBRAS/SAMBA before being renamed in honor of Max Planck, Nobel Prize winner for physics in 1918 and the originator of quantum theory.

Planck was launched with the Herschel observatory in May 2009 and soon separated from Herschel, beginning its primary mission objective, to map an all-sky survey, in February 2010. Along with the Herschel space observatory, Planck took up position in orbit in the L2 region of the Earth-Sun system, positioning itself here for optimum viewing. This positioning allows Planck to avoid stray light that might block the dim CMB radiation. While all-sky maps have been made before, Planck's CMB technology allows the observatory to view the oldest

light in the universe, dating back an incredible 13.7 billion years, with unprecedented accuracy. The telescope can also map areas of cold dust where new stars are on the brink of coming into existence.

The masses of information Planck is able to return to Earth builds upon those made by the NASA Wilkinson Microwave Anisotropy Probe (WMAP), which was launched in 2001 and carried out nine years of observations. WMAP in turn built upon NASA's Cosmic Background Explorer (COBE) satellite in the 1990s. Planck's data was superior in that it could measure anisotropies at higher resolution and sensitivities than WMAP, resulting in the enhanced data and quality of images sent back to earth.

As well as the all-sky survey, Planck's main mission objectives included studying how stars and galaxies form, as well as the process by which the universe came to life following the Big Bang

and the conditions that made evolution possible. Planck is also able to study all constituents of the universe in greater detail than ever, adding valuable pieces of information to the many questions surrounding the birth and formation of the universe.

The Planck telescope consists of a primary mirror that is 4.9 feet (1.5 m) in diameter, made of a carbon-fiber-reinforced plastic, which makes it durable enough to withstand much of the stresses and temperature differences of its launch. Planck was decommissioned in January 2012 when supplies of its liquid helium coolant ran out. Some equipment was still able to function, so certain scientific operations continued until October 2013. Planck was finally sent into heliocentric orbit before being deactivated on October 23, 2013.

STAYING COOL

Planck was fitted with a cryogenic coolant system allowing it to maintain an incredible temperature of 0.1 degrees above absolute zero. The optimum temperature has to remain stable for Planck to work efficiently, meaning that an increase of less than one degree could affect the equipment. The cooling system consists of a passive system, which uses thermal shields to precool the coolant. This coolant then goes through a three-stage process in the active cooling system. While the Low Frequency Instrument (LFI) could function at a slightly higher temperature, the High Frequency Instrument (HFI) cannot function without the constant supply of coolant to maintain these temperatures.

NUSTAR TELESCOPE

The NASA Nuclear Spectroscopic Telescope Array (NuSTAR) mission uses X-ray technology combined with the first orbiting telescope. Its primary purpose is to map regions of the sky for analysis of massive black holes, collapsed stars, supernova remnants, and the movement of particles in active galaxies. Launched as part of NASA's Small Explorer satellite program (SMEX-11), NuSTAR is able to study regions of the electromagnetic spectrum by focusing light which allows it to view high energy X-rays. In addition, NuSTAR is able to adapt its gaze in the case of unexpected supernovae and gamma-ray bursts almost as they occur.

BLACK HOLES

COMPARING BLACK HOLES . . . . MASS

SUPERMASSIVE BLACK HOLE . . . . 105 TO 1010 SOLAR MASSES
INTERMEDIATE BLACK HOLE . . . . 100 TO 105 SOLAR MASSES

BLACK HOLES OF ALL SIZES

Launched on June 13, 2012 by a Pegasus XL rocket, which itself was dropped from an L-1011 spacecraft—known as "Stargazer"—NuSTAR was soon able to send back data on ten supermassive black holes. One such black hole is thought to be present in the Milky Way galaxy—as well as most spiral and elliptical galaxies—in the area known as Sagittarius A in the center of our galaxy. While black holes can be tiny in size, especially when compared to their mass, supermassive black holes can hold the mass of over one million suns. NuSTAR has not yet discovered any new black holes, but its high resolution telescope means it can see high-energy X-ray light through the masses of dust and gas that surround black holes to a degree that no telescope ever has. Due to this, NuSTAR is able to shed new light on many questions surrounding the black hole, building on previous data sent from NASA's Chandra Observatory, which launched in 1999 and is still ongoing.

One of NuSTAR's capabilities is to respond to sudden occurrences in space, which the telescope can then be quickly aimed at to track. This very thing happened in April 2013 in the Milky Way, when flares near the middle of our galaxy lit up for hours. In another serendipitous example, NuSTAR was already observing Markarian 421 in the Ursa Major ("Great Bear") constellation when it observed a brightening of up to fifty times the normal levels. Markarian 421 is classed as a blazar—a galaxy with a supermassive black hole that actively sucks in matter. This feeding causes the black holes to light up and eject streams of energy and materials, which are sometimes directed at Earth.

Selected as the eleventh Small Explorer mission in January 2005, the NuSTAR mission was canceled a year later due to cuts in the NASA science budget. It was not until September 2007 that the program was again green-lighted, with a proposed launch date of August 2011. The initial two-year mission was due to be completed in June 2014, but was extended until 2016 so that NuSTAR can continue to send back new information on black holes and how they work.

EYES IN THE SKY

NuSTAR is equipped with a Wolter telescope built specifically with optics for viewing X-rays. The telescope was the brainchild of Hans Wolter (1911–78), who proposed three ways of using X-ray mirrors in telescopes in 1952. These mirrors are known as grazing incidence mirrors and they have a low plane of reflection. While these mirrors give a focused

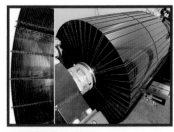

WOLTER'S WORK
The Wolter telescope focuses the high energy X-rays emitted by objects in space, allowing for the accurate observation of collapsed stars and black holes.

view of X-rays, the view of the light is limited. Wolter therefore proposed using two mirrors to widen the field of view and catch more light. The NuSTAR Wolter telescope employs two of these mirrors or optics, which are made up of concentric shells to maximize reflectivity. Wolter telescopes have been used in similar X-ray telescopes, such as the Chandra Observatory and the SWIFT Gamma-Ray Burst Mission launched by NASA in 2004.

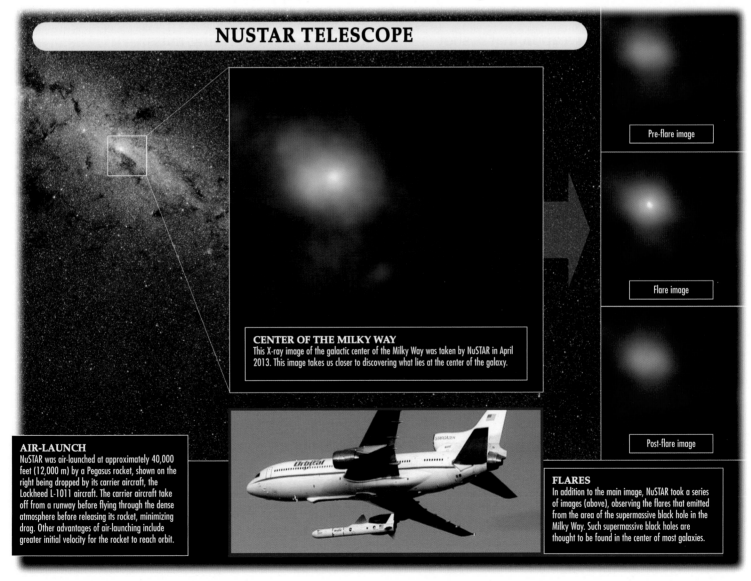

NUSTAR TELESCOPE

CENTER OF THE MILKY WAY
This X-ray image of the galactic center of the Milky Way was taken by NuSTAR in April 2013. This image takes us closer to discovering what lies at the center of the galaxy.

Pre-flare image

Flare image

Post-flare image

AIR-LAUNCH
NuSTAR was air-launched at approximately 40,000 feet (12,000 m) by a Pegasus rocket, shown on the right being dropped by its carrier aircraft, the Lockheed L-1011 aircraft. The carrier aircraft take off from a runway before flying through the dense atmosphere before releasing its rocket, minimizing drag. Other advantages of air-launching include greater initial velocity for the rocket to reach orbit.

FLARES
In addition to the main image, NuSTAR took a series of images (above), observing the flares that emitted from the area of the supermassive black hole in the Milky Way. Such supermassive black holes are thought to be found in the center of most galaxies.

GLOSSARY

aerobrake To decelerate (as a spacecraft) by passage through a planetary atmosphere.

aeroshell A protective casing that surrounds a spacecraft during reentry into the Earth's atmosphere.

apogee The point in outer space where an object traveling around the Earth, like the Moon or a satellite, is farthest away from the Earth.

autonomous Undertaken or carried on without outside control or influence.

ballistic missile A weapon that is shot through the sky over a great distance and then falls to the ground and explodes.

base station A relay located at the center of any of the cells of a cellular telephone system.

blazar A region at the center of a galaxy that sends out powerful jets of radiation in the direction of the Earth.

corona The thin, outermost part of the atmosphere of a star, such as the Sun.

cosmic microwave background radiation The microwave radiation spread throughout the universe that is the principal evidence supporting the Big Bang theory.

cosmic ray A stream of energy that enters the Earth's atmosphere from outer space

cryogenic Being or relating to very low temperatures.

ecliptic The great circle of the celestial sphere on which the Sun appears to move among the stars.

gamma ray A ray that is like an X-ray but has higher energy and that is given off particularly by a radioactive substance.

gravitational field The space around an object having mass in which the object's gravitational influence can be observed and measured.

gravitational wave A wave propagated in a gravitational field, predicted to occur as a result of an accelerating mass.

heliocentric Having or relating to the Sun as the center.

hermetic Closed tightly so that no air can go in or out.

infrared Producing or using rays of light that cannot be seen and that are longer than rays that produce red light.

jettison A voluntary discharge of cargo to lighten a ship's load.

magnetosphere A region of space surrounding a celestial object, such as a planet or star, that is dominated by the object's magnetic field so that charged particles are trapped in it.

microbial Describing an extremely small living thing that can only be viewed with a microscope.

microwave In physics, a very short wave of electromagnetic energy.

neutron star A dense celestial object that consists primarily of closely packed neutrons and that results from the collapse of a much larger stellar body.

orbit To travel around something, such as a planet or the Moon, in a curved path.

payload The things, such as passengers or bombs, that are carried by an aircraft or spacecraft.

perigee The point in outer space where an object traveling around the Earth, such as a satellite or the Moon, is closest to the Earth.

photopolarimeter An instrument used to measure the intensity and polarization of reflected light.

probe A device used to penetrate or send back information especially from outer space or a celestial body.

quantum theory A theory in physics that is based on the idea that energy (such as light) is made of small separate units of energy.

radiation belt A layer of energetic charged particles that are held in place around a magnetized planet.

retrorocket A reserve rocket engine (as on a spacecraft) used in decelerating.

sky map A chart showing the positions of celestial bodies in the sky.

solar flare A sudden temporary outburst of energy from a small area of the Sun's surface; also called a flare.

solar panel A large, flat piece of equipment that uses the Sun's light or heat to create electricity.

stratification The state of having many layers.

supernova The explosion of a star that causes the star to become extremely bright.

thruster A small rocket engine on a spacecraft, used to make alterations in its flight path or altitude.

transmitter A device that sends out radio or television signals.

xenon gas A colorless, chemical gas that is often used in electric lights.

FURTHER INFORMATION

BOOKS

Aldrin, Buzz. *Mission to Mars*. Washington, DC: National Geographic Society, 2014.

deGrasse Tyson, Neil. *Space Chronicles: Facing the Ultimate Frontier*. New York: W.W. Norton & Company, 2013.

Dickinson, Terence. *Hubble's Universe and Latest Images*. Toronto, Canada: Firefly Books, 2014.

Dinwiddie, Robert. *The Planets*. New York: DK, 2014.

Manning, Rob, and William L. Simon. *Mars Rover Curiosity: An Inside Account from Curiosity's Chief Engineer*. Washington, DC: Smithsonian Books, 2014.

WEBSITES

The *Curiosity* Mars Rover
www.nasa.gov/mission_pages/msl/index.html
Learn all about the Red Planet and view stunning photos taken by the *Curiosity* rover.

The ESA Planck Observatory
sci.esa.int/planck
This website provides a comprehensive overview of the Planck Observatory, its launch, its mission, and up-to-date data findings.

NASA's History of Animals in Space
history.nasa.gov/animals.html
On this site, NASA provides a detailed history of animals that have traveled into space.

New Horizons Probe Mission
www.nasa.gov/mission_pages/newhorizons/main/index.html
Follow the *New Horizons* probe as it explores the dwarf planet Pluto and the surrounding solar system.

The Smithsonian National Air and Space Museum's Online Space Race exhibition
airandspace.si.edu/exhibitions/space-race/online/index.htm
Learn all about the race to space between the United States and the former Soviet Union. Explore the challenges, triumphs, and failures that propelled space exploration ahead.

INDEX